THE LEGACY OF ZECHARIA SITCHIN

The Shifting Paradigm

M. J. EVANS, Ph.D.

Foreword by Paul Tice

Appendix by Jack Barranger

THE BOOK TREE
San Diego, California

ISBN 978-1-58509-533-9

Cover layout by
Toni Villalas

Cover photo
by Lena Jacobson

Published by
The Book Tree
P O Box 16476
San Diego, CA 92176
www.thebooktree.com
We provide fascinating and educational products to help awaken the public to new ideas and
information that would not be available otherwise.
Call 1 (800) 700-8733 for our FREE BOOK TREE CATALOG.

DEDICATION

Dedicated to the memory of Zecharia Sitchin

(the name "Zecharia" means "God remembers")

CONTENTS

FOREWORD

by Paul Tice

Zecharia Sitchin created a huge following with his books, which were translated into at least 26 languages. His general thesis is that mankind owes its genetic and cultural development to the outside intervention of an advanced race that visited Earth thousands of years ago.

The major goals of a true visionary are, in part, to provide new knowledge and to create positive change in the world. Zecharia Sitchin was such a visionary. He has left a body of work that has been embraced by millions around the world who form a powerful following, but the work has yet to be appreciated, understood or accepted by the majority of mainstream scientists or the general masses. The new knowledge is there, but the positive change that Sitchin has given birth to has not yet reached maturity. It may take more time before it unfolds... but many believe it will come and that a new paradigm is on the horizon.

Sitchin has helped to change the way we understand ourselves, where we came from and where we are going. As time goes by, more will find his work and reach these conclusions for themselves. His work centers on the idea that the mythologies of the ancient past were not just stories, but were depictions of authentic, real-life events. We have found this to be true in the case of Troy and the Trojan War, when the city of Troy was discovered in Western Turkey by Heinrich Schliemann in 1873, after he read the tale and became inspired enough to find it's true location. This was at a time when people believed it to be nothing more than a mythical story.

I was one of Sitchin's personal videographers on many trips around the world from 1996 to 1999, and was the publisher of one of his books (*Of Heaven and Earth*). I was with Sitchin when he visited Troy and numerous other sites around the world, in an effort to confirm the truth of such "mythical" stories. In Israel we went to what was believed to be the walls of Jericho and observed the strata, which reveals a discolored band of blackened ash when the city was burned at the approximate time the walls were supposed to have come down. We traveled into eastern Turkey where certain areas were considered hostile at the time – and we did experience some hostility – but we chose to venture there because in ancient times this part of Turkey was Northern Mesopotamia, the cradle of civilization, and the presumed home of the Anunnaki "gods." This is where the creation myths were born, which we investigated further. We explored the great lands of Egypt and the Mayan regions of Central America, investigating the stories of their gods. We traveled into a very dangerous part of Israel, the Golan Heights, seeking an important ancient site from as early as 4500 BC called Gilgal Refaim, the Stonehenge of the Middle East. The increased danger of encountering land mines, evidenced by occasional large craters and warning signs in three different languages, forced us to turn back. It was the only time I ever saw Sitchin retreat from his passion – but it had to be done for our safety.

When in Egypt in 1997, Sitchin had obtained permission to privately enter the Great Pyramid with the sole purpose of proving, once and for all, that the date of its construction was far earlier than currently accepted. This would also bring into question who the actual designers and builders were – something the Egyptians take great pride in. Yet Egyptians today (as well as mankind itself) cannot duplicate the building of such a sizable monument, having retained no information on reconstructing what they so readily take credit for.

The authorities reconsidered their decision, stalled Sitchin, but finally decided to save face and allow him entry. At the last minute they denied any photography, despite being accompanied by his still photographer, Wally Motloch, originally cleared for that purpose, and Abbas Nadim of Visions Travel. At the crucial moment inside the pyramid, when Sitchin had to climb a ladder toward reaching the proper area, an Egyptian "workman" dropped a large block of wood from above that hit Zecharia squarely on the head and knocked him down. Dazed and bleeding profusely, he was rushed immediately to a hospital. The point is, Sitchin knew how to prove the pyramid's dating, as explained more fully in his book, *Journeys to the Mythical Past*. He was stopped. Out of the thousands upon thousands of people to enter this structure, why is it that the one person who gets hit on the head and put into a life threatening situation is Zecharia Sitchin? Was this just a coincidence? These workmen were likely legitimate but in his account, Sitchin never said what they were doing in the pyramid. He was clearly suspicious of them and the authorities who had spoken with them shortly before the incident. Fearing for his safety, Sitchin left Egypt as soon as he was able to. I arrived on a slightly later flight than he had, and was left with instructions on where to go and what to videotape for him in Egypt, which was done. Sitchin was known as a great researcher and a clear threat to the status quo.

Sitchin could decipher the first known writing on earth, cuneiform script. We made sure to visit every museum we could on our journeys, and it was amazing to have a camera angled over his shoulder as he discovered a new script or cylinder seal and translated its meaning right there, as we went along.

There are those who have attacked Sitchin's interpretations as shared in his books, claiming that he made them fit his theories. Some have spent much time attacking Sitchin, because other interpretations can be made to show variance and bring attention to themselves. Translating Sumerian cuneiform can be an intricate business, having been more difficult for Sitchin without the recent knowledge we have today, but Zecharia worked hard at being accurate. He was not out to hoodwink anyone; he was totally and completely dedicated to uncovering the truth as he saw it.

I once recommended that he look into the work of Christian O'Brien, author of such works as *The Genius of the Few: The Story of those Who Founded the Garden of Eden* and *The Shining Ones*, among others. He was a British researcher who could also translate Sumerian cuneiform and came to the same general conclusions as Sitchin, as stunning as they were, but had reached them completely independent of him. They were unaware of each other's work while they conducted their research. Sitchin, however, responded to my recommendation by stating flatly that he no longer read or investigated the work of others. He did not want the work of others to taint his own intensely focused research in any way. During this same time (1996 to the early 2000's) he also gave up sitting on discussion panels and attending any seminars other than his own, although this changed during the last few years of his life. He was so focused on his work that he wanted others to receive his information in the same focused way. It was not about censoring others – it was about a serious intensity to teach and have others learn, without all the distractions that can muddle up the message.

In his earlier years, however, Sitchin studied the works of Samuel Noah Kramer quite seriously (as O'Brien had done), and called him his mentor. Kramer was a professor of Assyriology at the University of

Pennsylvania for many years in the mid-20th Century, and was known as the greatest Sumerian scholar of his time. If you read between the lines in many of Kramer's books, you may conclude that he knew some of what Sitchin later expanded upon – but Kramer, being in the strict, conservative world of academia, could not share these views openly at that time. Sitchin took what he learned from Kramer and was able to go beyond it to reach startling new conclusions – and finally say what Kramer may have wished he could have said without the fear of academic or professional repercussions.

Sitchin's critics are free to attack him as they will, because it has been found that he did make his share of mistakes. But this happens to many pioneers who blaze new trails. His savvy critics fail to include O'Brien in their attacks – a man who provides strong, independent corroboration of Sitchin's general thesis. Exploring new areas may cause mistakes to be made, but that can be expected. Sitchin's contributions far outweigh his flaws. It is better to make the journey and risk a few mistakes, than to leave everyone completely ignorant and in the dark.

The attacks on Sitchin have come from a number of camps. He has been accused of being a shape-shifting reptilian creature, along with former president George W. Bush and a host of other dignitaries. There was a claim or two that Sitchin was actually seen turning into one. Virtually every Sitchin follower has heard of this nonsense. When theories began to surface claiming that the ancient gods who visited Earth were reptilian in nature, Sitchin objected, telling them to simply look at the temple walls throughout the world, at the actual depictions of the "gods" that were made at the time, and you will see that they were all in human form – appearing generally like us. But the reptilian camp would have none of this. Since Sitchin did not agree with them, well, obviously, he had to *be* one of those dreaded reptilians. Why else would he refute such a claim (other than by using common sense)? In my three years of travel with Sitchin, throughout many countries of the world, not once at breakfast did he ever grow a tail and turn around and smash tables and chairs with it, causing people to run for their lives. Zecharia just wanted toast and eggs. He was never interested in snacking on fellow humans and none of the people on his trips ever disappeared.

Sitchin was a quiet, soft spoken, and very humble man. He was not loud or overbearing and did his best to avoid confrontation. I never saw him argue. He would always turn and walk the other way; it was a waste of time and energy. His modest demeanor could fool you into thinking that he was not as brilliant, tenacious and focused as he was.

He always remained quietly informed. During our travels he had to have his copy of the New York Times newspaper every day and would go to great lengths to arrange its delivery. He would get up early and read it thoroughly every morning. When they finally ran a special piece on him a few years later, it meant a great deal to him and he was very proud of it.

It was an honor to have known and worked with Sitchin. In 1995 I learned that he was leading an expedition to Central America to explore the Mayan ruins. When I found there was still room available to go, I spent virtually every last penny I had and joined the trip. It was the best ten days of my life. We explored Palenque, Teotihuacan, the Olmecs in Veracruz, Uxmal, Chichen Itza, Kabah and Dibilchaltun, the oldest known Mayan site. During the trip Sitchin asked what I did so I told him that I owned a small publishing company. Two months later he surprised me with a phone call, asking if I would publish a book for him. We made the initial plans and *Of Heaven and Earth* was born.

During further conversations Sitchin learned that I had 15 years of TV production experience and he wanted someone to video tape the many trips he had planned. I had just moved my publishing company to San Diego and was working with a large foundation that was capable of funding such an operation. Before his next excursion I was able to obtain a complete line of professional quality, portable equipment and enlisted a friend, Tedd St. Rain, to complete Sitchin's personal production "crew." We remained in business with him for the next three years, in both video production work and publishing. We privately published a history of Sitchin's family, in very limited supply for his family only, which was never released to the public.

On the many trips we videotaped, we agreed to film whatever Zecharia required and to give each tape to him immediately after it was shot, after we had dated and labeled them accordingly. Up until these trips, Sitchin had only line drawings and a few grainy pictures in his books – but now he would be getting video footage of all the major sites covered in his numerous works. And being in his late 70's at the time, he wanted

At work with Sitchin   photo by Fritz Meyer

this done before he was too old to travel. I was part of Zecharia's final journeys, documenting it all, and was determined to do a great job. Later, he would try to sell a show or series of shows to various cable networks, but they never met his price or requirements for control over final content. He told me that if no one met his terms, he didn't care – the tapes would be stored in his dresser drawer at home and that would be the end of it. He had worked hard for many years and believed he had earned enough respect to command a good price for his work and to put it together in the way he saw fit. Unfortunately, it was a dream that he failed to realize. It is hoped that someday, through whatever means that remain, we will be able to see these journeys with Sitchin unfold in "real time," other than in his books, as they are part of his legacy.

In the meantime, an overview of his legacy is being presented in this book. There is no better person I know who could write it than M. J. Evans, Ph.D., who contributed an important chapter in the first Sitchin book we published, called *Of Heaven and Earth*. That book consists of the transcripts that were presented at the First Sitchin Studies Day, held on October 6, 1996 in Denver, Colorado. Sitchin not only edited the book, he was the keynote speaker and therefore wrote the first 30 pages, followed by six others who supported his work. In this volume, for the first time, Sitchin experienced public support from respected Ph.D.'s in academia because two of them, Dr. Madeleine Briskin from the University of Cincinnati and Dr. M. J. Evans, contributed chapters. It meant a lot to Zecharia at the time to get such prestigious support. The other contributors were Neil Freer, Antonio Huneeus, Father Charles Moore and V. Susan Ferguson. M. J. Evans not only helped to give Sitchin the recognition he deserved from higher academic circles at that time, but is now, with this book, presenting a complete overview of important contributions made through his life's work.

This is a very thorough book and a fitting tribute to Sitchin. The few points not covered by the main text are included in a brief Appendix by Jack Barranger, which used the original title of this book when first written as a booklet in 1996. Jack is a retired professor of Critical Thinking, author of the *Past Shock* trilogy and the upcoming *When the Gods Return*. They did not intend to collaborate, but as it turns out, two retired college professors have combined forces to present to you, the reader, this tribute to the memory and work of Zecharia Sitchin.

Paul Tice

ACKNOWLEDGEMENTS

On October 9, 2010 Zecharia Sitchin passed through the veil that separates Heaven and Earth, leaving his family, friends, and hundred of "fans" who hold warm personal memories of his generosity in sharing with them his friendship and expertise. He will be greatly missed by all who knew, loved, admired and respected him. His published works now become a treasured legacy for his extensive world-wide audience.

My most heartfelt gratitude for the motivation that gave impetus to this book goes to Zecharia Sitchin who graciously invited me to participate in the First Sitchin Studies Day event held in 1996. The presentations that filled that day-long event are published under the title, *Of Heaven and Earth*. This invitation conveyed his interest in my ideas about the future impacts of his works, and became a turning point in my academic career. Over the past fifteen years of our friendship I came to value his indomitable spirit, his curiosity, and his unrelenting research efforts. I am fortunate to have traveled with him on several of his expeditions, and attended his seminars. I built a keen appreciation for the scope and depth of his expertise, and his steadfast adherence to his research findings. He has been an inspiration to me through the years, and my admiration of the man and his works informs this volume designed to celebrate his vast contribution.

Several of Zecharia's "fans" have shared a personal tribute to his role as friend, teacher and scholar, which can be read in the Afterword of this book. I am grateful to all those who contributed their photos, and whose names will appear with each one displayed. I greatly appreciate the encouragement and friendship of all my Sitchinite friends, and want to especially thank Barry, David, Joyce, Lena, Suzie, Jennifer, Wally, Fritz, and Sergio and Gaye Lub, who have been especially helpful. I also want to thank Paul Tice, another Sitchin friend and publisher at The Book Tree, who continues to be supportive of my ideas, and is a most generous and helpful editor.

Finally, to my family who now will know what I have been doing all these years when I spoke about my research and work on the book I planned to write – a most heartfelt thanks for your loving support.

PREFACE

Curiosity is one of the permanent
and certain characteristics
of a vigorous intellect.

—Samuel Johnson

Are we alone in the Universe? This is a question that has come to the mind of millions who have gazed up into the night sky. This question came to have particular relevance in America in the mid-twentieth century. On July 2, 1947 an unidentified flying object – carrying "alien" beings – is reported to have crashed near Roswell, New Mexico. While controversy has surrounded this incident – and continues to do so – this event brought the topic of extraterrestrial contact with Planet Earth to the forefront of public awareness.

However, Zecharia Sitchin's curiosity fueled his exploration of this challenging question well before the Roswell event. A life-long scholar of ancient languages, Sitchin built considerable expertise from his re-reading and close study of the Sumerian tablets. In those ancient texts he found evidence of an incredible story, one that is distinctly different from that published in the works of the first translators and scholars. This material, Sitchin believed, was not merely the mythological beliefs of the Sumerian people, but an historical record of a small group of space travelers who came to Earth thousands of years ago in vehicles that today we would identify as UFOs. This evidence, told to the Sumerians and scribed on clay tablets, was imbedded in the tablet materials. It indicated that these space travelers came from a planet whose elliptical orbit brought it from deep space into the vicinity of Earth to orbit our Sun, returning approximately every thirty-six hundred years. Sitchin's analysis of the tablet material proved to him – and through his books, to thousands of readers – that we are *not* alone in the Universe.

Sumerian clay tablet containing cuneiform writing on it's edges and the image of at least one god (left). Images like this, as opposed to hand-written tablets, were created when a cylinder seal (right) was rolled in clay.

photo courtesy of Gaye and Sergio Lub

The tablet evidence told that these explorers had productive and lasting impacts on Earth's civilizations, and especially on the origins of the human species. The conclusions Sitchin drew from the tablet evidence stood in direct contradiction to all the previously published interpretations of these materials. But Sitchin's belief in the validity of his conclusions was so strong that he moved from study to writing and finally publication of his findings. By the early 1970s, he had amassed such a wealth of material that he mapped out a series of books that he put forward under the designation *The Earth Chronicles*.

Sitchin's vocation as a journalist in Palestine during World War II without doubt honed his writing talent and when his books came forward, they engendered considerable public appreciation. Since his first publication in 1976 titled *The 12th Planet*, Sitchin's writings have filled fourteen books, and his conference presentations and seminars in which he sets out his findings with enviable logic, have reached thousands of curious individuals.

In a paper Zecharia Sitchin wrote in 1991 explaining the essence of his findings, titled *The 12th Planet: Key to the UFO Enigma*, he states: "I suggest to you that the answers to the UFO enigma lie in the ancient records of the existence of a 12th planet that belongs to our solar system." Sitchin goes further in an interview with UFO researcher Antonio Huneeus,[1] to say:

> Anyone who thinks that the UFO phenomenon began in 1947 with the Roswell incident, just doesn't know history, because the experience of mankind with so-called unidentified flying objects, which I say were in ancient times IFOs, *identified flying objects*, because the people in antiquity had no doubt that they knew what they were, what they represented and who operated them. It goes back to the beginning of mankind's recorded experiences…20, 25, 30,000 years [ago] almost to the beginning of the spread of Cro-Magnon man.[2]

My first encounter with Zecharia Sitchin came at the end of a two-day conference convened in Washington DC in May of 1995 by the Human Potential Foundation. The conference title, "When Cosmic Cultures Meet," was of keen interest to me as I had been exploring futures topics like building human habitats in space (otherwise called space colonies). I then was a member of relevant organizations that kept me abreast of new space-related events and furthered my interest in the field of future studies. Among them were the World Future Society, National Space Institute, the L-5 Society, and the International Association for New Sciences. The promotional material for the Human Potential conference listed several experts whose presentations I wanted to hear. Twenty-three notable speakers were listed as presenters, all of whom were distinguished in the fields of human consciousness, ET contact and UFOs. These were the arenas where study of ET contact and its impact were underway. Among the presenters were the late John Mack, MD from Harvard's Medical School faculty who studied the experiences of abductees; James J. Hurtak, Ph.D. who founded the Academy for Future Science and was senior scientific consultant for Advanced Scientific Systems; R. Leo Sprinkle, Ph.D. a counseling psychologist who worked with UFO experiencers; and John L. Petersen, a futurist and founder of The Arlington Institute think tank. At the outset of that conference, I never had even heard of Zecharia Sitchin.

On the last day of the well-attended gathering, Mr. Sitchin spoke as a contributor to a panel dealing with future perspectives. In a masterfully crafted and succinct summary, he laid out the essence of his historically oriented message, which set the stage for his final comments on future implications. He mentioned that he was one of only 200 scholars who could read the ancient Sumerian clay tablets. His study of Sumerian and other ancient languages – Akkadian, Babylonian, and early Hebrew – also informed his interpretation of the veiled information contained in the tablets. What he mined from those texts was that a group of technologically advanced space travelers have been repeatedly coming to and going from Earth to their planet for almost half a million years. He further states:

> They had a space base or way station on Mars, and I think all that which is past is significant not only to the future ... but also to the present. If you want to understand what is going on nowadays and what we could expect [it is] that we are not alone... in our own solar system. [3]

Because Sitchin's expertise is extensive, it masks his little recognized entertaining sense of humor. It was in the opening sentences of his presentation that I got my first glimpse of his inventiveness, delivered in what I later learned was his inimitable straight-faced manner. He told of a question posed to him by a conference attendee who asked if, when he made his presentation, he would use English or Sumerian. He assured the questioner, that he would talk in English. However he added:

> Because having been born in Russia and raised in Palestine, educated in England and lived in the United States, I don't know what kind of English I'm talking by now. But I trust it is understandable. [4]

He went on to comment on his reaction to the scientific effort known as the SETI (the Search for Extraterrestrial Intelligence) research.

> I almost chuckle when I see this search continuing. They are not looking for other beings, they are looking for intelligence. In other words, rocks that are clever or some such other thing. They don't dare even say "intelligent beings," but [ironically] they are looking for them OUT THERE, not near us. [5]

This subtle but engaging quality of Sitchin's personality gave me the courage to approach this impressive speaker at the end of this session. I went to the podium and introduced myself. I had formed a question during his impressively informative presentation that stemmed from my recent study of ancient sites in Ireland. In gathering background for that study, I had read the Irish myth that recounted the indigenous peoples' encounter with the Tuatha de Danann, an ancient tribe who splashed down on the coast of Ireland and engaged the indigenous peoples in three battles. These events are chronicled in the Irish legend known as *The Battle of Moytura*.[6] According to this legend, these invaders used *magic* on the battlefield to win their first two battles. In the third, their magic waned, causing them to lose. According to some sources, these people left the island, migrating to some unknown place that may have been in the Near East.[7]

From Mr. Sitchin I wanted to know if there was any possibility that these ancient peoples – the Tuatha de Danann, who held the intention of settling on the island we now call Ireland – were the same ancient ones he wrote about, the space travelers he said the Sumerians called the Anunnaki (those who to Earth from heaven came). Mr. Sitchin's answer to my question was: "Read my books."

I took seriously this directive, and devoted the summer of 1995 to reading Sitchin's (then) six books. Being trained as an academic, I am *not* inclined to accept without an in-depth evaluation, new, provocative information. Because his work was so intriguing, I decided to explore Sitchin's sources, with the purpose of evaluating for myself his body of work to determine if it was creditable scholarship. I studied the redactions and translations as well as the interpretations of the several original scholars he cited. I re-studied Sitchin's references to determine if he used academic sources accurately, and sought to determine if his discussion was logically plausible and internally consistent. I quickly realized that to take issue with Sitchin's interpretations of the Sumerian cuneiform texts (including differentiating the translation of specific words that were drawn from Akkadian and Babylonian versions of the same texts) one would need to learn the Sumerian and these subsequent languages. Beyond that imposing and impossible (for me) task, one would need to rely on the work of the early redactors, translators, and scholarly interpretations. I did find, as a reasonable but flawed substitute for gaining access to the most famous tales: the Internet was a resource giving English translations of many of the most well known translated Sumerian texts.

What I learned after a summer of study was that the Sitchin information indeed was well grounded in legitimate sources. Most importantly, his literary style was engaging, coherent, and logical. I had to keep reminding myself throughout this verification process that Sitchin's approach was informed by his space-age mindset, and that his approach to the ancient texts assumed them to be the recorded *history* of the Anunnaki – not myth, legend or the religious beliefs of the Sumerian people. As one might expect, given the original interpretations of the tablets were set out well before the full impact of our scientific space-age, Sitchin's interpretations of the translated texts were very different from those of the original scholars. Importantly, his scientific evidence was compelling, covering as it does several fields of study. I came to more fully understand the thematic clue he published on the front cover of his 1990 book, *Genesis Revisited*, which indicated the book would answer the question: "Is Modern Science Catching Up With Ancient Knowledge?"

I ended my study efforts over that summer with sufficient grounds to question my initial skepticism. Because I still was not fully convinced that I could completely accept some topics included in Sitchin's body of work without further study, I continued to explore whatever relevant literature I could find. The deeper I probed, the more persuaded I became that Sitchin's work was valid, and I realized that I could not find any flaws to support a rejection stance. In fact, without realizing it at that time, I found myself accepting Sitchin's body of work – albeit tentatively.

My next step was to contact Mr. Sitchin and suggest a personal meeting in which I could pose to him several questions. He graciously accommodated my request, and we enjoyed a pleasant lunch in New York City in the early Spring of 1996. Without disclosing my efforts to challenge the validity of his work, his forthright responses to my several questions brought me to further appreciate this unpretentious man's accumulated knowledge and expertise.

In late May/early June of the summer of 1996, I elected to travel with Mr. Sitchin and a group of his "fans" (his descriptor for those who supported his work) on an excursion that included visiting ancient sites and museums in Greece, and on the islands of Santorini and Crete.[8] On that trip, I had the opportunity to talk at length with others who knew well Sitchin's work, many who had traveled with him several times on previous journeys to the Middle East and Middle and South America. I came to appreciate the enthusiasm and excitement Sitchin's work held for my fellow travelers, who incidentally came from all walks of life (i.e. lawyers, airline pilots, nuclear scientists, engineers, auto factory workers, writers, and business owners, just to name a few). This trip also provided me with an opportunity to become better acquainted with Mr. Sitchin. If any skepticism lingered in my mind, this event served to push it well into the back of my mind.

In mid-summer of that year, Zecharia (I now counted myself among his travel friends) called to invited me to participate in an event to be held in Denver in October to be called the First Sitchin Studies Day. Five others whose work acknowledged Sitchin's findings – and Sitchin himself – contributed to the day-long program. In preparing my presentation, I found myself remembering the psychological process I went through during my first encounter with his books. In the final version of my paper I chose to discuss a *positive encounter psychology*, meaning a psychological reaction emerging from an acceptance of his work as an almost intuitive response. Such a stance did not necessarily mean the reader held full acceptance of all the material, but did hold a mindset that considered it plausible. In addition, having introduced Sitchin's books to several people following my own initial encounter, I learned from interviews with those readers that some did *not* accept his findings. This information informed my paper's discussion and analysis of a *negative encounter psychology*. The results of my findings of the impact of the Sitchin material on most of these new readers led me to realize his work represented a new paradigm – a new way of conceptualizing the origins of Earth's civilization and the origin of the human species. I subsequently titled that presentation "The Paradigm Has Shifted: What's Next?" It appears as the third chapter in the published conference presentations. These proceedings are titled *Of Heaven and Earth*. Sitchin edited this book and contributed the first chapter.

My close study of Sitchin's work continued as each of his subsequent books came forward. I also traveled with him on a few more of his journeys, namely to Israel, the British Museum/Malta, and Italy. My university teaching responsibilities precluded my ability to participate in the Sitchin group trips to Syria/Lebanon, Turkey, and Mexico, experiences I now regret missing. However, I did attend one conference held in the Yucatan where he was a speaker, and we visited two ancient sites together: Dzibilchaltun, considered to be the oldest Mayan city, and Chichen Itza, which means "Dew of Water that Poses on the Mouth of the Sacred Well, Abode of the Lord of Good Rain."[9]

Criticism of Sitchin's ideas and work is to be expected in the context of the skeptical and debunker mindsets that prevail in today's society, and which, unfortunately, are widely circulated as a result of the forum provided by the Internet. However, two unusual extra-planetary events lend credence to Sitchin's discussions. These events tell us that something unusual is going on *out there*.

In 1988-89 two Russian space probes met their demise as they approached Phobos, a Martian moon. The first apparently was destroyed as it did not transmit anything. On March 28, 1989 the second probe's camera showed an object approaching the probe just before the camera picture went black. Russian ground controllers released close-up infrared photos showing an object that cast a shadow on the Martian surface. The Russians commented on this observation in these words: "It is an object which shouldn't have been there." When I saw this shadow image, it looked to me like a UFO. The speculation that came forward concluded that the Russian mission had been deliberately terminated by *aliens* unwilling to allow either of these Phobos probes to approach that Martian moon.

The demise of these two exploratory Russian probes offers convincing evidence that somebody, likely extraterrestrials, are *again* operating in our solar system, specifically on Mars. Sitchin announced this conclusion at the Human Potential Foundation conference, and again in one of his other conference presentations. He reiterates his belief that Mars is again in use and deals with this as fact in his book *The End of Days*. In that discussion, he states that an alien avant-garde presence (probably robotic) is using Phobos – and perhaps Mars itself – as a way-station.[10]

Coupled with the sightings of Planet X (the designation given by astronomers to a very large planetary object coming out of deep space) and confirmation of this planet's existence made by a U.S. Naval Observatory scientist, Robert Harrington, who worked collaboratively with astronomer and physicist Tom Van Flandern, a specialist in celestial mechanics, we have legitimate scientific data on which to seriously consider the veracity of Sitchin's conclusions about another planet belonging to our solar system. The Planet X information was published in the news media on December 30, 1983.

Now the challenge is to establish whether Planet X is the Anunnaki planet called *Nibiru*, the home planet of the ancient space travelers. Only events yet to unfold in the future will confirm – or disprove – the conclusions explaining the Phobos incident, and provide confirmation to document that Planet X actually is Nibiru.   Most provocatively, confirmation of the return of Nibiru also would bring the Anunnaki into range to again visit Earth. More will be discussed about this very real possibility in chapter five.

Whatever criticisms are launched against the validity of Sitchin's findings, these criticisms, to be legitimate, must deal directly with the volumes of physical evidence presented in Sitchin's books.   But, the likelihood of any of the critics taking the time and putting forth the effort to "walk in Sitchin's footsteps," is, in Sitchin's own published words – a "fat chance."[11]

INTRODUCTION

Some things are true whether you believe them–or not.

—Dialogue by character Nathan Messenger,
played by Dennis Franz,
in the movie *The City of Angels.* [12]

Who was Zecharia Sitchin? What is the substance of his contribution? We assert that his collected works shift the existing explanatory paradigm and ostensibly rewrite ancient history. What are the grounds on which this assertion stands? Most importantly, what are the future implications of Sitchin's work? These are questions we will examine in this book.

While much has been written by and about Zecharia Sitchin, there still is more to say. To begin, he was a soft spoken, unassuming man of incredible intellect who devoted his life to sharing the amazing story he found when he studied the ancient Sumerian clay tablets discovered over a century ago in Mesopotamia. Sitchin came to interpret the ancient clay tablets after he spent years studying ancient languages. He applied his accumulated knowledge to re-interpreting the ancient texts which contained, among other things, stories about beings from another planet who first came to Earth some 445,000 years ago and returned several times. He also studied the works of the early scholars who discovered, translated, redacted, and interpreted these tablet materials. As he plodded through this demanding work, he began to see that these texts held recognizable modern characteristics. To enrich his textual research, he visited numerous prestigious museum collections that held artifact evidence in support of his conclusions. Interestingly, Sitchin found that many of these museum artifacts were mislabeled, probably because museum curators had no basis for fully understanding their enigmatic qualities and space traveler relationships.

We confidently assert that Sitchin's contribution shifts the existing explanatory paradigm, thereby giving a new understanding to the origins of Earth's civilizations, to human origins, and to the sudden appearance of civilization on Earth. To address this assertion, we first must ask: Does Sitchin's contribution indeed do this? For newly interpreted information to shift the existing paradigm, the information must map unexplored territory, answer numerous existing questions, and provide illumination into how – and where – to collect new data. We will look into the evidence that supports this assumption.

The original linguists who studied the ancient tablets made assumptions about what the stories contained on the ancient tablets said. Sitchin found himself drawing *different* interpretations than did those early scholars because he was looking at the material *through our modern space age lens.* He saw the tablet accounts as records of a group of sentient beings (called in the tablets the Anunnaki) who were technologically advanced space explorers. They came to Earth on a mission to locate, mine, and transship gold back to their planet, to be used there to preserve their diminishing atmosphere. Early in their sojourn here these space travelers were forced to deal with a mutiny of the small crew assigned to labor in the extremely deep gold mines. To deal with this problem, the leaders of this Earth expedition made use of their advanced scientific knowledge to genetically engineer docile workers.[13] The end result of several genetic experiments eventually led to the creation of the human species, accomplished by merging their own genes with those of a hominid already existing here on this planet. All this information mapped new territory in 1976 when Sitchin's first book, *The 12th Planet,* was published.

Sitchin's books provide a plethora of supporting evidence. He cites numerous sources throughout his books, all of which can be examined by skeptical readers ambitious enough to search out and read his sources for themselves. A little known fact is that the first manuscript submitted of *The 12th Planet* book contained nearly three times the number of references that appear in the final publication. The publisher's editors advised him to reduce that original number to make the book more palatable to a public readership.

Sitchin (center) with travel group in Xalapa, Mexico
photo courtesy of Lena Jacobson

That Zecharia Sitchin was an extraordinary and extremely knowledgeable man can be attested to by the thousands who have attended his numerous in-person presentations. And those who have accompanied him on his several expeditions to places important to documenting the validity of phenomena he discusses in his books, have found these trips to be not only memorable, but extraordinary learning experiences.[14] His in-depth knowledge of ancient sites is noteworthy because it illuminates a plethora of details about the places where ancient as well as historic events took place. On the other hand, for those who only know Sitchin through his books, his writing distinguishes him as a formidable researcher and an extremely talented writer. His books have brought to light a highly believable explanation of the information scribed in clay thousands of years ago. When we seriously engage the implications of Sitchin's interpretations, we learn who we are and how we came to be living on Planet Earth.

Ancient clay tablet with Sumerian writing   Photo courtesy of Gaye & Sergio Lub

In actuality, the story Sitchin found on these ancient clay tablets is quite understandable to all of us because it contains concepts that now have become commonplace in the modern space age in which we live. These concepts involve travel through space, the landing and take off of space vehicles from Earth, space probes into the outer reaches of our solar system, and advanced scientific knowledge about how to perform genetic manipulation. However, scholars of the late 19th and early 20th centuries who were the first tablet translators, redactors, and interpreters, struggled to explain information they found perplexing and seemingly imaginary. Thus, they surmised that the tablets contained the *legends, religious beliefs* and *mythical stories* of the cultures in which they were found – the Sumerian, Akkadian, and Babylonian cultures. Sitchin, on the other hand, in his fourteen books,[15] which incidentally are highly accepted and praised around the world, put forward an uncommon and remarkably different interpretation by comparison. His books documented the activities and exploits of these space travelers as well as their contributions to Earth's inhabitants.

These findings enlarged the curiosity of numerous subsequent researchers. In essence, Sitchin research efforts, findings, and documentation of often obscure sources opened a conceptual framework that others have followed. John Casti, an historian of science, gives us an appropriate signal of the impact of new perspectives resulting from a shifted paradigm (though not referring specifically to Sitchin's work). He tells us that the one who shifts the paradigm generates a new generation of thinking "explorers" who " ... accept the new vision of 'truth.' Through these new glasses, [they] see a whole new set of puzzles to be solved..." [16] This is the personal impact of Sitchin's work on hundreds of his readers.

In Sitchin's publications he points out that, unlike other scholars, he did *not* consider the cuneiform text stories to be *myth*. Instead, in the manner of a genuine "out of the box" thinker, he posed these questions: "What if these texts are *not* myths? What if all these tales really happened?" He carried this mindset as he wrote, and also when he traveled to many sites in the Near East, Mexico and South America where he located physical evidence that supported his findings. His books also use our modern space-age science to interpret the ancient evidence. It is his detailed evidence of ancient texts interpreted with modern science that is the key to why the contribution of Zecharia Sitchin is so exceptional, so valuable, and so important for modern times.

This book's discussion looks at the implications of the Sitchin findings and conclusions. These implications are provocation for expanding our thinking about the future. Along the way, it is useful to look at how the Sitchin information contributes to our cultural fabric and how it impacts modern scientific and cultural thought. In the discussion that unfolds below, we explore the evidence that helps us understand why, at the time the tablets were discovered and translated, those who wrote and published their interpretations of these texts *assumed* them to be describing the legends, religious beliefs and mythical stories of the Sumerian people. [17] Here we look closely at the role of *myth*, as this concept is the original theoretical umbrella under which the tablet stories first were set forth. Much of the difficulty those who reject Sitchin's work have in accepting his explanations, likely derives from the fact that mythology is a widespread body of interpretation and holds a credible place in the academic study of ancient history and literature.

In this discussion we celebrate the contributions embedded in Sitchin's volumes. The overarching impact of his work gives substance to the assertion that the work of Zecharia Sitchin moves the frontiers of our knowledge so far forward that it greatly enlarges the scope of explanation of ancient history. Our discussion explains a multitude of unanswered questions, such as: how a complex civilization suddenly appears in Mesopotamia, points to who the people were who built the many mega stone structures found around the world, and most provocatively, looks a how modern homo sapiens bridge the gap between ancient humans and the modern sentient human species.

To illuminate what is meant by a shifted paradigm, we will examine the *concept of a paradigm*, and provide evidence in support of the assertion that Sitchin's work is so provocative and coherent that it indeed shifts the paradigm. The pre-Sitchin explanatory framework was posited prior to the space age, whereas Sitchin's explanations make logical sense under the modern scientific developments that abound in our technologically informed space-oriented age.

When Sitchin's material is encountered, it provokes two types of response – one of acceptance, and another of rejection. We will analyze these reactions to better understand them, and to lay out insights into why the "deniers" of the validity of Sitchin's work attack it in the critical and even malicious ways they do. Then we will look into the future impact of Sitchin's work, and its future implications.

To publish a completely different explanation of previously well studied interpretations, as Sitchin has done, requires considerable *intellectual bravery*, a quality which Sitchin wore humbly. Intellectual bravery has been an important characteristic of the truly creative thinkers throughout history who have made valuable contributions to our platform of knowledge by pushing the frontiers of knowledge forward. Many – if not most – of these creative thinkers have faced criticism, and their work initially has been met with disdain, rejection, and even censure.[18] For the most part, time has proven these brave scholars' ideas to be viewed, after subsequent analysis, to be valid contributions.

As one might expect, Sitchin also has detractors. However, trusting the thoroughness of his research and the accuracy of his conclusions, built as they are upon tangible evidence, Sitchin tolerated these detractors with non-engagement.

He held firm to his belief that the reinterpreted messages of the tablets not only are understandable to a modern audience, but they have validity and authority when conceptualized within the scientific dimensions of our contemporary society. Moreover, he has explained who built many – if not all – of the enigmatic features that are found around the world, evidence that remains on the landscape for anyone willing to travel to consider for themselves. Sitchin guided groups of "fans" to sites to see for themselves these unusual features. One can read about these expeditions in his two informative books.[19] Taking interested people to view landscape evidence has generated a vocal body of Sitchin supporters who bring their understandings back to share with even wider audiences.

Sitchin group at the Oracle Stone, Delphi Museum
photo by Visions Travel

As a result of Sitchin's curiosity, perseverance, courage, confidence, and considerable writing talent, thousands now have a new explanatory paradigm to consider, one that serves as a tool to greatly enlarge mindsets of readers around the world, and informs the ideas we will carry into the future. Through Sitchin's books, we have access to a previously unrecognized explanation of first explorers, and now know their planet exists so that we can look for its return in the foreseeable future.[20] We also can understand the origin of our species – homo sapiens sapiens – and from where our civilization originated. These and numerous additional understandings have made a remarkable impact on modern society, set out by a brave and indomitable researcher and scholar – Zecharia Sitchin.

CHAPTER ONE

THE SUMERIAN TABLETS AS MYTH

Ancient myths were stories [used by] our forebears to assimilate the mysteries that occurred around and within them.

—From *The World of Myth* by David Adams Leeming

There is no such thing as an "empirical" observation; we always see by interpretation, and the interpretation we use is given by the prevailing paradigm of the moment.

—John L. Casti's *Paradigms Lost: Images of Man in the Mirror of Science*

When the first scholars redacted the cuneiform scripts found on the ancient clay tablets, they saw a mythical quality in these texts, and to explain them, they drew on the interpretive tradition prevalent at the time of the discovery of these artifacts. They made assumptions based on these perceived mythical qualities, which set a precedent by establishing the assumption that the tablet stories were myths. This mythological interpretive label was used thereafter to derive and convey the meaning of these texts, a tradition that still operates today. These scholars' assumptions were drawn from the cultural context that held sway at the time they carried out their analytical work. Because the tablets were proved to be very ancient artifacts, the most prevalent assumption was that the stories set out the beliefs that dominated the thinking of the Sumerian society. The original scholars who worked with these texts considered the tablet stories to be the folk stories, allegories, sagas, or even parables believed by these people. Through time, these ancient materials became classified mostly as *myth*.

Understandability is an important characteristic to be sought when working with information derived from the Sumerian tablets. It is the quality under which this type of material gains its integrity and makes its greatest contribution.   Labeling ancient materials as *myth* stems from the period we know as the Enlightenment. Following that period, and into the late 19th and early 20th centuries (the periods when the tablets first were discovered and interpreted), myths were thought to be simpleminded stories born in the fantasies and beliefs of the ancient peoples. Interestingly, this is a common understanding of the meaning of the word *myth* in most people's minds today.   We must remind ourselves that the word *myth* is the word used by academic and lay writers alike. It is *not* the label used by source cultures to classify their own stories.

The early scholars likely were bewildered by a large amount of the information in the tablets, especially that discussing their gods. These scholars no doubt seriously struggled to make the best sense possible within their cultural frame of reference. Likely they decided that they certainly were not reading history.[21] Even if they did initially consider the material history, and still could not make sense of portions of it, they reassessed this initial judgment. Instead, they considered the tablet stories to be allegory, or even sagas and parables. However, by using the label *myth*, they could "explain away" content that was not understandable, and once that label was used, it hid under its protective wing many – if not all – other possible interpretations.

Drawing on the work done on *myth* by Bronislaw Malinowski, a well known myth theorist, we find that the word *myth* is used to mark a particular category of story. In his view, *myth* referred not to just any story, but to a particular class of story, one that "...primarily meant a radiant and important story."[22] When Malinowski analyzed the utility of *myth*, he indicated that it functioned unconsciously as far as the actors in question are concerned.[23] Interestingly, there was little scribed in the Sumerian tablets that were "unconscious" to the Sumerian scribes. They put on clay what they learned from, or was dictated to them by the space travelers.

The role of *myth* as it has been studied and interpreted across history is varied. Some published discussions see *myth* as a mode of expression recounting early human efforts to deal with mysteries inherent in natural phenomena, and indicate it points toward the early people's efforts to connect with seemingly magical forces they observed in the natural world. Works by Edith Hamilton and Johan Gottfried Herder are presumed to fall into this category. Others categorize different types of myth that appear to function as *philosophical* or *artistic* expression. C. G. Heyne, a German scholar, indicates that *artistic* myths are, for example, the works of Homer and Hesiod. On the other hand, stories that explained the causes and origins of phenomena comprise the category he called *philosophical* myth.[24] Philosophical myth explicates beliefs, particularly that content which was ascribed to the supernatural realm of nature.

Myth, then, is the category of information that appears to have served as a "catch all" container into which was thrown most tablet translations, especially when the content was not understood. Often this label was used when the text dealt with "things superhuman" or the behavior of beings labeled "gods." Robert Graves, a scholar of Hebrew myth, observed that the book of *Genesis* is seen to "…harbour vestigial accounts of gods and goddesses – disguised as men, women, angels, monsters, or demons."[25] These stories carried a powerful message. They were – and still are – presumed to represented a fantasy world in which the early peoples lived, a world based on emotion that embraced magic, make-believe, and religious constructs. The gods of mythology were deemed to be all-powerful, and possessed of magical powers – like flight. This type of interpretation has led to all sorts of modern extrapolations which draw on archaic interpretations of the information. Much academic work would need to be re-conceptualized if Sitchin's interpretations were fully understood and accepted.

Additionally, *myth* has been clearly differentiated from fable, folktale, and saga.[26] Saga, in the view of Gerhard von Rad, a German Lutheran pastor and Old Testament scholar, was a particularly important literary form. He indicates that "History acts as an enemy of saga: it threatens it, it waylays it, it slanders it and perverts the words." He goes further to say: "There often is an entire world of events – actually experienced events – enclosed in a single saga."[27] Without the benefit of these definitions, it would be easy to designate both myth and saga as the same, or at least similar. These definitions allow us to see that these labels cannot be used interchangeably. According to von Rad, saga holds a higher density than history. History supposedly "… records exactly and trustworthily everything that saga mentions unclearly and typically with distortion."[28] Some might consider that much of the Sumerian material belongs to the saga category – but not Zecharia Sitchin. Sitchin's belief was that the tablet materials indeed were history.

Once the details of the tablets were classified under the category of *myth*, this concept seems to have become the lens through which all subsequent analyses were viewed. This is seen over and over again in the works that fall into the mythology tradition. In dealing with Babylonian material in 1880, George Smith, a renowned assyriologist, best remembered for discovering and translating the *Epic of Gilgamesh*, tells us that Sumerian "… mythology was local in origin; each of the gods had a particular city which was the focus of the people's worship." Smith goes on to say, "In some remote age there appears to have been three great cities in the county: Erich, Eridu, and Nipur."[29] Smith was working with the tablet material that he assumed was the religious focus on these cities. Because he believed that the "gods" were *ethereal*, he probably was confused as to how early cities could command a worshipful focus, when in fact, it was the Anunnaki leaders who built and inhabited these cities who were being shown adoration, according to Sitchin.

We can better understand Smith's assumptions by reading Sitchin's explanations. Sitchin tells us is that each city was the abode of a different Anunnaki leader. Erech (Uruk) was the place set aside for Anu (the king on the Anunnaki's home planet, Nibiru) and his spouse, Antu. This city was built for these royals to use when they came to Earth from their home planet – a journey they did occasionally make.

Eridu, meaning in Sumerian "House in the Faraway Built," was the first settlement and the home in Mesopotamia of Enki, first-born son of Anu; and Nipur was the pre-diluvial Mission Control Center where Enlil (the rightful son of Anu born of Anu's sister[30]) maintained his link with the planet Nibiru.[31]

Anu's sons, Enki and Enlil, were the Anunnaki leaders of the Earth-based missions, and often are mentioned by name in the Sumerian tablet material. But, Smith recognized only that the theme of the texts focused on "gods," and to him that implied supernatural beings. The idea of beings referred to as "gods" *living on Earth* was probably unfathomable to Smith. His confusion is understandable, given the comparative limitations of his world view at the time of his writing. But, according to Sitchin, the Anunnaki not only built but dwelled in these cities. Because the Anunnaki were perceived as superior to their "created" ones, they indeed were the objects of worship.

It is useful here to briefly explore the way the tablet texts refer to "gods," although Sitchin does this in considerable detail in his books. Many early scholars assumed that a belief in many gods preoccupied the Sumerians (and the Akkadians and Babylonians who followed them). This belief is reported by scholar Louis Delaporte, who wrote about Mesopotamia. He states, "…the Sumero-Akkadians admitted the existence of a great number of deities who were all celestial beings." He struggled to explain other observed phenomena, as we see when he goes on to say, "…the supreme god, Anu, was the god of sky."[32] We now know, from Sitchin's interpretations, that Anu was king on the planet Nibiru, and did indeed live "up there." Because the possibility of "coming down" from another planet (or from outer space) held no recognizable reality before the 20th century, such material in the texts confounded the early scholars. Delaporte also tells us that the Sumerian peoples "…attributed to their deities the virtues and passions of humanity, and endowed them with the same modes of life as were found on Earth, but raised their "gods" above mankind by conferring immortality upon them."[33] This scholar also decided that the tablets implied the "gods" of the Sumerians had superhuman qualities as well. Indeed, the Sumerian people revered the Anunnaki who had "created" them and who obviously exhibited extraordinary capabilities.

Sitchin tells us that one of the Anunnaki leaders, Enki, *did* have passions, and he is reported (in the tablets) to have liberally indulged in these physical passions. Furthermore, the Anunnaki *did* live long lives. The Anunnaki measured time in *sars*, which were the 3600 earth year intervals it took their planet to make one revolution around our sun.[34] And, it is quite possible that the Anunnaki indeed appeared different as a result of the fact they lived what we would call extremely extended lifespans. The Anunnaki evidenced some additional physical qualities, which made their faces appear different from the earthlings they created (exhibiting a glow).[35] The tablets may have suggested these differences, but the early redactors were unable to interpret these clues ascribed to the "gods" probably because the scholars believed the gods to be ethereal beings. Sitchin's material unravels some of the puzzlement held by the early scholars, allowing us to see through what we now can refer to as the "misunderstandings" of the redactors. However, the early scholars reconciled their perplexity by classing all the tablet stories as *myth*.

If we look closely at a well-known story, namely the Sumerian *Myth of Creation*, set out on seven tablets, we can see more clearly how the distortion prompting the classification of the tablets as *myth* seemed logical to the early redactors. What we now know is that the *Enuma Elish*, known as the *Epic of Creation*, used the word "gods" as a translation for the word Sitchin found to mean *planet*. Once Sitchin saw the solar system formation process described in this material, we can legitimately call the older translations "misinterpretations."[36] However, the first redactors assumed the word "gods" referred to a large array of *ethereal* and *mythical* "gods."[37] We need to remember that it was Sitchin"s space-age mindset that permitted him to unravel such confusion and put forth an accurate meaning of this story. Writers in the 18th and 19th centuries were schooled in Greek and Roman beliefs and were familiar with the concept of *polytheism*. References to multiple "gods" (little "g") in the texts permitted the early scholars to assume that the Sumerians worshiped many gods. We now can better understand the reasons behind the early scholars' struggles to make sense of this story, *now that we have the benefit of Sitchin's explanations.*

Let us examine a few of the actual lines of Leonard King's redaction of the *Enuma Elish* – that he calls a legend – giving particular attention to the way the words "god" or "gods" appear:

> *1. When in the height heaven was not named,*
> *2. And the earth beneath did not yet bear a name,*
> *3. And the primeval Absu, who begat them,*
> *4. Chaos, Tiamat, the mother of them both, –*
> *5. Their waters were mingled together,*
> *6. And no field was formed, no marsh was to be seen;*
> *7. When the gods none had been called into being,*
> *8. And none bore a name, and no destinies [were ordained]*
> *9. Then were created the gods in the midst of [heaven]*

Keeping in mind that in line 7 where the word "gods" appears, and using Sitchin's interpretation, we can see that this word refers to the fact that no planets yet has been spun off the Sun. In line 9, the text states that the "gods" were created in the heavens – as indeed was the case when we interpret the word "gods" as planets. The text ascribes "human-like" qualities and gender to the entities under discussion. These entities (planets) also each were given names:

> *10. Lahmu and Lahamu were called into being*
> *12. Ansar and Kisar were created, and over them*
> *17. Nudimmud, whom his fathers [his] begatters*
> *18. Abounding in all wisdom,*
> *19. He was exceeding strong*
> *20. He had no rival*
> *21. (Thus) were established ... the great gods*[38]

To fully understand the original text, one needs to read it in the original form.[39] However, when Sitchin, at first studied it, no doubt he also puzzled over what this text was describing. Perhaps it was the reference to a "battle" between each entity that began to suggest to Sitchin some astronomical formative process, particularly when the text discussed a large body (referring to Absu, (the Sun) *spewing out* matter that formed these entities and which seemed to interact in violent ways between themselves. The similarity to the way planetary scientists described the formation of planets around a distant star (sun) likely became the key idea that explained what the Sumerian epic was recounting. Sitchin's interpretive lens allowed him to see a logical scientific similarity – one understandably conceptually out of reach to the original redactors.

Recent planetary explorations provide us with the means to understand the ancient text. The epic also indicates that prior to the events described, no "objects" existed in the beginning (line 7), and then, one by one, ejections from Absu (the sun) *begat* material that became the revered entities. The end result was that the story described the entire formative process of the Solar system. Even though, in Sitchin's mind, his new interpretation was a very different one from that given by the early redactors, he boldly set it out in his book, *The 12th Planet*. What we now know is: *this information is not a legend; it tells us the story of the origin of our solar system.*

Another problem the redactors must have struggled to understand deals with the use of descriptive labels, which refer to "gods" who *lived* on Earth. When used in interpreting other later texts, the same word that appears in the *Enuma Elish* referring to planets also was used to refer to the *actual* beings who brought this information to planet Earth. We can appreciate the translator's confusion.

Perhaps we can derive a better understanding of the original scholars' confusion by examining the use of a few other words derived from the translations. Two of the first earth-based leaders of the Anunnaki, Enki and Enlil, sons of the planet Nibiru's king, Anu, were believed to be ethereal "gods" by the redactors. What we now know (based on Sitchin's work) is that these two Anunnaki were actual personages sent to Earth to administer and carry out the Anunnaki reasons for coming here. Each was assigned to a different Earth mission, and carried a descriptive name that used the word "lord." Such a worshipful designation easily would have implied (to the redactors) that these entities were objects of religious reverence. Enki was given the title "*Lord* of Earth" and Enlil was designated "*Lord* of the Command." These appellations implied to Sitchin that Enki and Enlil were *not* ethereal beings. We have no detail on the quandaries of these early scholars, but one thing is for certain: Enlil and Enki were, in our modern vernacular, the "supreme commanders."

A fascinating story discussed in the *Enuma Elish* emerged after Sitchin decoded that text. The origins of the full array of planetary objects were laid out, and each entity given names in the ancient text which we do not recognize now, because we call them by their modern names: *Ansar* was the name given to Saturn; *Kishar* is Jupiter; *Nudimmud* is Neptune; *Lahmu* is Mars; and *Lahamu* is Venus. As each planet was spun off from the Sun, it interacted violently with the existing planetary bodies. It was the electromagnetic and gravitational events that occurred in the formative eras of the solar system that generated Sitchin's use of the word "battle." This descriptor likely contributed to the shift in Sitchin's interpretative perspective, having learned from his study of modern science how a sun behaves to form planets around it. The electromagnetic effects of planetary proximity created enormous lightening discharges such as those described in the "coded" terms of this ancient story.[40] Sitchin devotes an entire chapter to "The Celestial Battle" in *The 12ᵗʰ Planet*. One point bears repeating: it was Sitchin's understanding of modern scientific information that informed his understanding of the *actual* meaning embedded in this text. When Sitchin substituted the word *planet* for "gods," the word used in the *Enuma Elish*, the mythological shroud that surrounded this ancient text fell away, no doubt prompting him to issue the following provocative explication – *Eureka!*

Of particular interest to us "earthlings" is the behavior of first planet formed. It was called *Tiamat* and originally orbited the sun, according to the ancient text, from a position between Jupiter and Mars. In the tablet narrative, Tiamat's body was *rent asunder* by the satellites of a mighty *intruder*, a large planetary body called *Marduk.*[41] The tablet narrative tells of numerous "battles" between Tiamat and Marduk's body and his moons, which occurred on the repeating incursions of Marduk into our solar system. A final "hit" by a moon of Marduk on one of his subsequent orbits was of sufficient force to shunt her[42] (Tiamat) into an orbital position "third from the Sun," leaving a space between Jupiter and Mars that has long perplexed planetary scientists whose calculations indicate another planet should have orbited there. This space now is known as "the asteroid belt" in modern planetary science terminology. We who have read Sitchin, now know that this location contains the fragmented residue of Tiamat. After achieving its new orbital location, this *fractured* planet was renamed *Earth*. In *The 12th Planet*, Sitchin's chapter on "The Celestial Battle" is a lesson in planetary science, recorded in ancient times, and describing events now under study in modern celestial science.

Scientists have long puzzled over the tumultuous behavior of the Earth's crust around and in the Pacific basin. This ocean basin is of particular interest to *this* discussion because it links us to this ancient knowledge. From Sitchin's interpretation of the *Enuma Elish* text, we now know that the Pacific basin is the scar in the planet's structure that resulted from the collision of Tiamat with Marduk and his moons. The interest of modern scientists in this part of Planet Earth is not to confirm the validity of the ancient knowledge, but (as one might expect) to further scientific understandings about Earth's structure, and to add more knowledge as to understanding the behavior of the tectonic plates that are located in and around the Pacific basin. *Our interest* focuses on what happened to Planet Earth – and continues to happen – because we now see that the origin of this area's tectonic behavior is explained in the ancient texts. Our interest brings us to the interface between modern science and ancient knowledge.

Let us look further into this interface. It was determined by geoscientists that there were shallow portions of Earth's crust where the molten mantle approaches – and even breaks through – the surface crust. During the International Geophysical Year of 1957-59, an exploratory project, called the Moho Project, was launched to measure the crust's

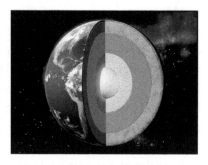

Earth cross-section

composition and thickness.[43] The exploration sites selected were in the Pacific basin. This part of the planet experiences enormous tectonic activity around its margins. Called "The Ring of Fire," the Pacific marginal zone has the highest number of earthquakes on the globe. It contains numerous volcanoes, as well as a particularly interesting "hot spot," where volcanic activity over millennia has created a particularly impressive group of islands. We know these volcanic remnants as the Hawaiian Islands.[44]

According to scientists, Mauna Loa, a famous volcano located on the southeastern-most island, has been erupting for at least 700,000 years. Another active volcano, Kilauea, located on the side of Mauna Loa, is estimated to have first erupted 300,000 or more years ago. It has a separate magna-pumping chamber, and has been actively spewing lava from the underlying since 1983 allowing the mantle to emerge to the surface continuously.

Using our understandings drawn from the ancient knowledge, we can put forward a tentative hypothesis: the enormous array of Pacific tectonic activity and volcanism results from the fracturing of the planet in the primordial and formative period of the solar system, as explained in the *Enuma Elish*. The crust, violently torn apart by the primordial impact, continues to be unstable and undergoes almost continuous adjustment. Moreover, the tear in the crust was deep enough that it nearly reached the mantle, leaving cracks that now function as volcanoes.

In one of his seminars, Sitchin showed a model of Planet Earth's continents "floating" on a transparent globe constructed with a wire-like framework that simulates lines of latitude and longitude.[45] This model makes the oceans of the globe transparent, but it clearly shows the enormity of the planet's damage from the primordial impact. What is significant for our understanding is that this cavity then filled with the waters that  prior to this cataclysmic event *covered the entire* Earth.[46] Sitchin's interpretation of the *Enuma Elish* offers modern science a plausible causative explanation for these tectonic phenomena.

In preparation for his first publication in 1976, Sitchin carried out years of scholarly research and preparation. He read, studied, and analyzed the works of the 19th and early 20th century scholars who first produced the translations and redactions of the ancient tablet artifacts.[47] These early scholars – whose exploratory expeditions were supported by famous universities and museums located in Europe and America – interpreted the tablet information under the then prevalent mythological hypothesis. Looking further into this now dated mythological interpretative tradition, we find an interesting perspective in the work of renowned scholar Joseph Campbell, whose expertise covers the study of the history of mythology around the world. Writing about ancient myth, he tells us that

> ... *myths* appear also in religious contexts, where they are accepted not only as factually true but even as revelations of the verities to which the whole culture is a living witness and from which it derives both its spiritual authority and its temporal power.[48]

Read in the context of Sitchin's findings, Campbell's interpretations strike a confirmatory note. Campbell likely was unfamiliar with

Sitchin's work, and he developed his interpretations while working with thousands of mythical stories found in numerous cultures around the world. It is only by an uncanny coincidence that his words support Sitchin's findings.

Corroboration for the type of conclusions that Sitchin's material presents also comes from another unaffiliated source. Anthropological researchers Michael Cremo and Richard Thompson, who have studied numerous examples of how academically trained researchers classified mythic material, point out that it was typical for traditionally educated researchers to *ignore* anything anomalous found in ancient material. This likely was common practice because the theory that informed the dominant explanatory hypothesis used by academics was one that drew on the legitimated mythology scholarship.[49] Anomalous material never was published in traditional academic journals, especially if the researcher's findings did not appear to build on previously published interpretations. It was mythic and religious belief themes that dominated analyses in the eras of greatest exploration, discovery, recovery and interpretation of artifacts and tablets from the ancient Near East civilizations. So, if any alternative explanations might have even occurred to traditional scholars writing in the 20th century, they never saw the "light of day."

Early in his work, Sitchin entertained the likelihood that what we now recognize as modern science was embedded in these ancient stories. Subsequently, he re-read these ancient materials with "new eyes." This type of awareness is called recognition of *anomalous evidence* by Cremo and Thompson. These researchers have collected numerous examples of controversial evidence that is ignored under the old accepted explanatory paradigm. When Sitchin came to his striking realizations, specifically that the ancient stories held in them implications of what we now can explain as modern technology – phenomena such as space travel, landings and take-offs of space vehicles, global monitoring capability, genetic manipulation, and knowledge of weapons of mass destruction – he published his books for the mass market readership.[50]

This has proved to be a fortuitous decision, one that has seen his books made available to audiences around the world. His works are published in at least twenty – if not more – different languages.[51] In retrospect, Sitchin's initial decision was instrumental in disseminating his findings to a world-wide audience.

It must be pointed out here that no "second hand" summary of Sitchin's discussions does justice to the highly readable and expertly crafted narratives written by Sitchin and published in his books. To obtain the full impact of his contribution one needs to read Sitchin's books for him or her self. Taken together, Sitchin's fourteen books comprise **an extraordinary scholarly contribution**.[52]

Sitchin's provocative and well-grounded findings have a profound impact on the minds of those who read – and will read – his books. One of the most important impacts of his entire body of work is that it shifts the explanations of concepts that allow us to explain the way we understand the history of the world. Thus we assert that Sitchin's explanations generate a new paradigm. We now will explore this new Sitchin paradigm in detail.

CHAPTER TWO

THE SITCHIN PARADIGM

You never change things by fighting the existing reality.
To change something, build a new model that makes
the existing model obsolete.

—R. Buckminster Fuller

The provocative nature of Zecharia Sitchin's work enlarges the scope of our understandings of ancient civilization by addressing the when, how, why and from where it originated. Once exposed to Sitchin's explanations, our way of understanding ancient history changes significantly. Most importantly, the Sitchin material leaves us with a wide array of implications for the future. The Sitchin information shakes up what we previously learned about the origins of religion, re-defines our understanding of the origins of the human species, and explains how early Earth inhabitants were guided to develop and implement the elements of civilization on this planet. In other words, Sitchin's work sets out a *new explanatory framework* that shapes our perceptions and gives us a much broader way of making meaning. This is what we here identify as the *Sitchin paradigm*.

The way we make meaning about the world around us involves drawing on a body of legitimated explanations we have absorbed over the years. These explanations, taken together, are called *paradigms*. A paradigm consists of a set of presuppositions that shape and direct the way we have learned to see, think about, and explain the world. These explanations function as a way to draw conclusions, build generalizations, and under these tenants, are used to solve puzzles (in the scientific sense). In doing these intellectual things, a paradigm provides us with a way of thinking about and understanding the world around us.[53] Sitchin's work *enlarges* these existing explanations, and derived as it is from the tangible evidence of the Sumerian tablets, sheds new light on the origins of Earth's past civilizations, and in particular, explains how modern humans came to inhabit Planet Earth.

The existing explanatory frameworks (paradigms) we draw on and have learned throughout our lives are called *normal science* by Thomas Kuhn,[54] a renowned historian of science and author of *The Structure of Scientific Revolutions.* Kuhn made an all-encompassing contribution to our understanding of the characteristics that define paradigms and what must happen for a new paradigm to be identified.

The paradigm *already* in place is based on past achievements, and through time has become widely acknowledged as "the way it is." It is known as *normal science.* These well understood ways of making meaning, then, are a bastion of accepted knowledge that takes on an aura of unassailability because it has been so widely accepted. While the explanations that normal science understandings provide are assumed to yield a legitimate way of seeing and understanding the world, functioning as they do as an overarching set of explanations, questions still remain under this existing body of explanation, questions that beg for attention and further study.

Mounting any challenge to the existing body of normal science holds potential for weakening the existing (old) paradigm. Kuhn lays the blame for a weakened old paradigm on an accumulation of anomalies – observations or explanations that previously appeared to fit under the old explanatory framework, but no longer do in light of new information. In a comparative perspective, the old explanations are inadequate or even incorrect. The old explanatory framework is in serious trouble when an ever growing body of different observations becomes known, and the sharp thinkers among us suddenly become converts to the legitimacy of the new information. Almost immediately, these converts seem to lose their confidence in the (old) traditional explanations, especially after they see the scope of the new ones. Alan Chalmers, an historian of science, goes further by indicating that a weakening of the existing paradigm occurs when new seemingly heretical ideas are even allowed onto the scene.[55]

Kuhn also points out an important characteristic of *normal science.* People are emotionally attached to it; it was their original first-learned explanatory framework, and only reluctantly – if at all – are those from this "old school" willing to give up their belief in these traditional ways of thinking in order to accept a new body of explanation. Many, who hear about a new way of explaining what they already know, hold tight to their accumulated knowledge. An entire defensive mindset is provoked when new information, which is – reluctantly – perceived to hold legitimacy, and enter the public arena. Because of its inherent logic, the *new* information is seen by those alert thinkers among us who are open to new ideas as being intuitively plausible and filled with explanatory power.

Because we all are identified – at first – with the *status quo,* some *perceive a threat* from the new body of explanation. Often the reaction of this group is characterized by an attack on the information, asserting it is invalid, improperly obtained, or incorrectly interpreted – or all three. Many among this non-accepting group make it their mission to launch an attack aimed at discrediting the information. We call these individuals skeptics and/or debunkers. If the strategies of these self-appointed experts[56] do not succeed in eliminating, or at least soundly discrediting the perceived threat of the new explanations, the debunkers turn their attack on the person who brings the new information into the public arena. These *ad hominine* attacks, which have little to do with the facts of the argument, can be malicious.

Kuhn helps us understand these supercritical and defensive reactions. He indicates that the logic that forces a shift away from the existing paradigm to a new stronger body of explanation requires one to *transfer allegiance* from one (the existing) way of viewing the world to another (new and different) way of thinking and perceiving. Giving up explanations that have worked – until now – requires an intellectual conversion experience that cannot be forced, in Kuhn's view.[57] Furthermore, those whose egos are invested in the realm of normal science and who have built their reputations expounding the traditional "tried and true" explanations, may never transfer their allegiance, and may even refuse to give due consideration to the new explanations. Kuhn gives a much stronger interpretation of the consequences to one who dares to challenge, redefine, or even just expand the existing body of knowledge when he points out that when scientific revolutions occur, they involve intellectual rather than liquid bloodshed of a similar order of magnitude to that found in the political arena. This is a fitting analogy to some of the attacks launched against Sitchin and his work.

Kuhn provides us with criteria to use to determine *if* a new paradigm indeed has been brought to the table. For a *new paradigm* to take hold, it must contain information and explanation provocative enough to be called *unprecedented.* It must attract a group of believers away from the existing explanations, and to do this, it must provide a *wider* scope of explanation; it must hold a rational format; and it must be internally consistant. At the same time, this new framework of explanation must be balanced, logical, and carefully grounded with data of unassailable validity. In other words, these data must be logically convincing, as well as factually verifiable.

Further, a new paradigm is expected to meet another of the conditions Kuhn lays out. It must hold considerable potential for responding to the numerous unanswered questions left by the existing explanatory frameworks, and it must be able to at least attack and perhaps even solve several other observed puzzles. For a new body of explanation to *shift the paradigm,* it must widen our understandings, answer heretofore unanswerable questions, and do so in such a credible way that it attracts and persuades intelligent, rational, open-minded thinkers to accept it. Let us see if Sitchin's work meets Kuhn's conditions and qualifies as a new explanatory framework that indeed *shifts the paradigm.*

The Kuhn criteria met by the Sitchin material focuses on the scope of Sitchin's documentation. One body of questions remaining from the old paradigm deals with the seemingly *sudden appearance* of the elements of civilization that are attributed to the Sumerians. How did the complex elements of a highly structured civilization emerge in Sumeria? The old explanations would tell us that these features of civilization were "invented" in ancient Sumer. Importantly, the work of Samuel Noah Kramer in his 1963 book, *The Sumerians*, presents a long list of *complex* structures that seemed to "just appear" in Sumer. Kramer discusses each key element that he calls "firsts."[58] These include: the first schools, the first bicameral congress, the first historian, the first pharmacopoeia, the first farmer's almanac, the first cosmogony, the first proverbs and sayings, the first literary debates, the first library catalog, and even the first Noah. The legal system, court system, and enforcement of justice, along with music, also have been shown by researchers to have originated in Sumer. It is important to note that Kramer's work predates Sitchin's first publication, so he had no knowledge of Sitchin's findings.[59] Attributing all these elements of a civilization to the inventiveness of the Sumerians is a flawed conclusion, one too important to the point made by Sitchin. These elements of civilization were *given* to the Sumerians. Joseph Campbell, the scholar famous for his study of mythology, also acknowledges the suddenness of the appearance of civilization in Sumer. He alludes to what we recognize as the crux of the Sitchin findings when he writes:

> The abruptness that characterized the entire Sumerian cultural syndrome has since constituted the germinal unit of all the high civilizations of the world .... The whole cultural syndrome that has since constituted the germinal unit of all of the high civilizations of the world ... we cannot attribute to any achievement of the mentality of simple peasants.... It was actually and clearly the highly conscious creation ... of the mind and science of a new order of humanity, which had never before appeared in the history of mankind.... [60]

This "know-how" to organize the complexities that characterize a civilized society, according to Sitchin's explanations, came from the Anunnaki space travelers who were the first inhabitants of the Mesopotamian region and "created" the Sumerians. The space travelers *brought* this knowledge to Earth. The Sitchin paradigm clearly indicates that Earth was a "visited" planet that was "seeded" and culturally cultivated by *other terrestrial* (OT) expertise.[61] In other words, the elements of civilization were *inserted.*

The explanatory information in place *before* Sitchin's work was published, implies that the components of early civilization came about through the inventiveness of the first humans who came to live in Mesopotamia. According to anthropologists, early man roamed the Earth, and engaged in hunting and gathering activities.[62] Most early scientific explanations imply that early peoples learned several important complicated civilizing constructs by such processes as "independent invention" and "trial and error." According to Sitchin's work, these explanations cannot be the explanations that apply to Sumer. Learning of complex structures needs either models (to promote learning by imitation), or direct instruction.[63]

Under the Sitchin paradigm, not only did the OTs *give* the constructs of civilization to the Sumerians, they taught those people skills and knowledge that emerged as fields of study: agriculture, hydrology, construction, architecture and astronomy.[64] We do not want to imply here that the Sumerian people were not intelligent, inventive, skilled, or industrious. In fact, they became the scribes who set down the Anunnaki stories on wet clay so they obviously were literate in the cuneiform script and language. They also recorded stories given them on thousands of clay tablets, including copious commercial transactions. They built settlements; they built palaces; they fashioned sculptures and what we now call artifacts (like the cylinder seals). They worked in metals; and perhaps (under Anunnaki direction) even built a spaceport and a landing platform for their space traveling ventures.[65]

Certainly Sitchin's well researched explanations are *unprecedented* when compared to what has been known and taught for years. Look at the outstanding features of Sitchin's contribution: he identified another planet that belongs to our solar system, the home world of technologically advanced beings that explored and colonized Earth and built settlements in Mesopotamia. Sitchin also tells us that it was these space travelers who genetically engineered a new species. He identified evidence that these OTs held advanced technological knowledge that, for example, facilitated their use of space vehicles to remotely monitor Earth for gold deposits, a substance they needed to save their home planet's diminishing atmosphere.

Sitchin with statue of ancient king of Mari, Ishtup-ilum, which some also believe to be a rendition of the Sumerian god, Enlil, in Aleppo, Syria

photo courtesy of Lena Jacobson

His explorations of ancient sites proved that these OTs built launch sites from which to transship the gold they mined here. All these achievements were uncovered by Sitchin's extensive research efforts.

Perhaps the most provocative component of Sitchin's material is the evidence indicating that these space travelers genetically engineered humans by "blending" the genes of one of their males with those of an existing female hominid. This certainly is a provocatively different explanation of human origins that was *unprecedented*, to say the least. The concept of genetic engineering served, according to Sitchin's information, to "jump-start" the development of human beings who were intelligent.

Zecharia with statue of mother goddess, Ninhursag, at Aleppo Museum, Syria. She and Enki, according to Sitchin, supervised the genetic alterations of man.

photo courtesy of Wally Motloch

Only in the late 20th century does modern science allow us to appreciate the concept of genetic engineering. In the ancient Sumerian text called *Atrahasis*, Sitchin found the ancient evidence of this concept, and an ancient cylinder seal found among hundreds of these clay records attests to the existence of a laboratory.[66] Many – if not most – of these developments likely would not even have been recognizable, let alone understood, by the early tablet redactors. From Sitchin's boldness in setting out coherent explanations of these contributions of the Anunnaki, we find the evidence that (in Sitchin's words), gives us the ability to appreciate that *"modern science is catching up with ancient knowledge."*[67]

Another of Kuhn's qualifications for a body of information to shift the paradigm is the development of a group of *converts* who accept the new explanatory model. These converts find the information able to provide answers to their longstanding questions. Sitchin has accumulated thousands of readers who see the legitimacy of the evidence he brings forward, and who accept his body of work as valid. His public talks and conference presentations during the more than thirty years following his first book's publication always drew large crowds. His overseas tours were well attended by a loyal group of people he calls "his fans," as well as first time travelers who had read Sitchin's books and wanted to see physical evidence on the landscape that supported Sitchin's findings for themselves.

After the turn of this century (in the 2000s) he conducted weekend seminars in major cities (such as Santa Fe, Los Angeles, Chicago, Philadelphia, and Dallas) and he always spoke to filled conference rooms. These throngs represented individuals who found Sitchin's publications enlightening, personally meaningful, and left a lasting and profound effect on their thinking. Additionally, his books have reached international audiences around the world (in translated versions where necessary) and have sold – and continue to sell – thousands of copies. The sheer number of individuals who have encountered Sitchin's explanations – and accept them – represents convincing evidence that a large group of "acceptors" exist who recognize Sitchin's explanations as logical and convincing. Based as his findings are on copious bodies of research, and presented with sound and observable evidence, the intellectually curious public seemingly has no problem accepting the inherent validity of his explanations.

Likely the Anunnaki also built the hundreds of mega structures still seen standing in various landscape settings. The purposes of these structures have baffled local residents and others interested in them for centuries. These enigmatic phenomena, consisting mostly of mega stone structures, can be seen in various places in western Europe, and elsewhere around the world. One interesting structure is called a dolmen. It typically consists of three huge upright stones and an equally huge capstone balanced on the uprights. Most dolmen are considered to be burial sites, even though, in most cases, never were skeletal remains found when they were excavated.[68] There are no records as to who built these enigmatic stone structures, and more importantly, no convincing explanations as to how the multi-ton stones were moved and raised has come forward.

View of Pentre Ifan dolmen looking east, showing the balancing of the south-facing capstone. Coast of Wales, near Fishguard.   Photo by author

The landscapes of Ireland, Wales and Brittany contain numerous dolmen that look like "space-age satellite dishes."[69] The capstones of these structures orient to the southwest,[70] and have been found to contain high levels of quartz. Our modern computer technology has demonstrated the enormous capability of quartz in facilitating communication and information storage. We can be properly curious as to what purpose these dolmen structures held for the ancient peoples – or for their builders. These structures are enigmas under the "old" explanatory paradigm and represent unanswered questions emerging from the old explanations. Sitchin's work gives us at least a plausible answer.

Stonehenge, Salisbury Plain in Southern England   Photo by author

Stonehenge and Avebury, both located in southern England, are well-known stone mega structures. In Ireland, another notable stone and earthen structure, one that predates Stonehenge by at least a thousand years, is known as Newgrange (called *Bru na Boinne* in the ancient Irish literature). This structure is a multi-layered mound, and originally was surrounded by a circle of huge standing stones. This unique mound is constructed with a passage leading into the mound, opening into a corbelled inner chamber. Radio carbon dating of this structure indicates its origins to be at least 5200 years old, making it older than the Great Pyramid in Egypt.

*Ancient Newgrange mound, located on north side of Boyne Valley,
County Meath, Ireland.*   Photo by author

*One of 97 kerbstones that ring the base of Newgrange mound. The carved spirals
appear on several kerbstones, as does the serrated pick dressing, below it.*

Photo by author

   Who the builders of Newgrange were still is a mystery to researchers.
The builders are attributed to each of a succession of peoples who
invaded Ireland over time, but the results of the dating procedures now
rule out all but the original inhabitants of the island. Irish researcher,
Martin Brennan, tells us that Newgrange was built by an ancient

tribe, the Tuatha de Danann, identified in stories contained in the Irish Mythological Cycle, a collection of ancient tales. He indicates that

> The Tuatha de Danann, [were] the earliest known native Irish *gods* disguised as a supernatural race of wizards and magicians, who *descended from the sky* and inhabited Ireland before the coming of the Celts. They have been referred to as The Lords of Light (italic emphasis mine) [71]

The archaeologist who performed the excavation and restoration of Newgrange, Professor Michael O'Kelly,[72] published a detailed report documenting his amazement at the intricacies he found when he performed the two-year restoration project that involved excavation and rebuilding this structure. A subsequent researcher amplifies O'Kelly's reactions by stating that the structure showed the "... skill, precision and planning ability of the Master Builder of Newgrange."[73] The original purpose of this enigmatic mound is thought to be astronomical; however this is only one possible explanation. Sitchin's body of work, explaining as it does the role of the Anunnaki in ancient history, provides a plausible explanation of who built this structure. While there is no direct proof that this landscape feature is associated with the Anunnaki, the reported mythological clues lead us to hypothesize that the Anunnaki most likely were the "master builders." What the Sitchin material does for us is to provide plausible conjectures as to who the ancient builders likely were who constructed these structures.

Another well-known, huge carved structure, the Sphinx, poses enigmatic questions as to its age and original purpose. Before the Egyptians applied stones and plaster to mask the evidence of water-borne erosion on the lower sides of the Sphinx (evidence of this erosion seen in the photo below), the explanations proffered as to who built the Sphinx and its age are attributed to the first dynasties that comprise Egyptian history.[74] Under the construct provided by the Sitchin paradigm, the date the Sphinx was built falls into a much older range, one that predates by millennia the well popularized Egyptian dates.

One can understand the efforts of the Egyptian antiquities experts to avoid any acknowledgement of Sitchin's discussions of the Sphinx as his information undermines their promulgated dates.[75] But, for those who are "in the know" (meaning accepting of Sitchin's material), the answer as to when the Sphinx was built and who built it strongly suggests it was the Anunnaki.

The Sphinx, located on the Giza Plateau in Cairo, Egypt.
Evidence of erosion clearly seen, lengthwise.

In Sitchin's book, *Journeys to the Mythical Past*, the color plates depict photos taken at several sites where ancient mega stone structures were visited by Sitchin and his "fans." These photos document some of the evidence that supports Sitchin's findings. For example, on the Maltese island of Gozo, the Sitchin group visited the megalithic temple complex called Ggantija. The group assembled next to an outer wall of the structure (see below) to demonstrate the enormous size of the stones used to construct two side by side temples at this site.

Perhaps the oldest and most famous temple structure on Malta is Hagar Qim, a temple of considerable complexity. A book titled *Malta's Prediluvian Culture at the Stone-Age Temples*, written by Joseph Ellul, an archaeologist and life-long resident of Malta, provides considerable information on the mega stone temples found on Malta. He makes the case for these stone megalithic structures to antedate the Great Flood (commonly called Noah's Flood).[76]

Sitchin "fans" at Hagar Qim temple wall in Malta, originally built between 2400-2200 B.C., showing enormous size of the stones.   Photo by Visions Travel

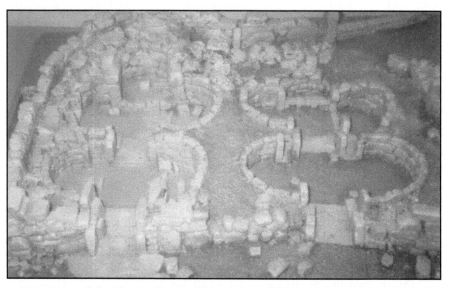

Museum model of the similar temple complex of Ggantija, located on Island of Gozo, near Malta, circa 2450 B.C.

Photo by author

In addition to these temples on the Maltese islands, another temple is purported to be submerged off the coast of these islands. The land around the existing three Maltese islands was inundated by *another* flood event caused when an ancient land bridge, connecting African and European landmasses, was weakened by a tectonic event. The enormous pressure of the Atlantic waters, which were reported to have been 6000 feet higher than the inland (Mediterranean) basin, spilled through creating the geologic structure we now know as the Straits of Gibraltar. This inundation created the current size of the Mediterranean Sea and the high ground that now is the Islands of Malta.

The obvious questions relative to the Malta mega stone structures are like those posed about the origins of the other mega stone phenomena. How old are these structures? Who built them? And what was their purpose for the builders? As to the age of the Malta temples, Ellul tells us that a visiting British archaeologist (unnamed in Ellul's book), claims to have studied prehistoric ruins around the Mediterranean, and he is reported to believe these structures on Malta to be some 12,000 years old.[77] Again, the Sitchin paradigm seems to offer a plausible explanation as to the builders.

As impressive as the Maltese temples are, the much more provocative mega stone structures that support Sitchin's findings are discussed in his book, *The Earth Chronicles Expeditions*. They are the mega stones blocks found at Baalbek in Lebanon.[78] We learn the purpose of the extraordinarily huge stone blocks, which are precisely cut and placed, from a prediluvian story titled *The Epic of Gilgamesh*.[79] These stone blocks are gigantic by comparison to other structures that use stones. This Baalbek site is identified in the ancient epic by two physical features – its cedar forest on a huge mountain.[80] Gilgamesh wanted to achieve immortality, a characteristic common to the Anunnaki. His mother was Anunnaki, but his father, a priest, was human. This combination made Gilgamesh two-thirds divine, so he felt he was entitled to this anti-death quality.[81] He was told of two locations where space vehicles were available, so he made what Sitchin calls the first of his "in-search-of" journeys to a place in the Cedar Mountains called the Landing Place.[82] The epic narrative indicates that this was a secret place of the gods. Gilgamesh was told he would find vehicles there that could take him to the planet Nibiru. It was only on the Planet Nibiru where the ability to have the Anunnaki characteristic of a long lifespan was possible.[83]

Huge stone at base of the Trilithon, Baalbak
photo courtesy of Gaye and Sergio Lub

The enormous foundation stone blocks seen at Baalbek were quarried very near the ancient landing site. A Roman temple was built on top of them, so ruins can be seen atop the ancient blocks. These massive stones are precisely cut to form a base platform that likely would have supported the launching of space vehicles. Three of these huge stone blocks are called The Trilithon. Each enormous block weighs more than 1100 tons, with relatively smaller blocks, weighing "only" (Sitchin's word) 500 tons each placed above them. These three blocks are touted to be the largest deliberately shaped stones in the world.[84] What is even more mysterious is the partially quarried huge block, already shaped like the ones in place, that partially emerges from the quarry floor.

Sitchin views partially quarried block at Baalbek, Lebanon, called the Stone of the Pregnant Woman, estimated to weigh over 1000 tons. An additional stone was found nearby in the 1990's, estimated to be 200 tons heavier.   Photo courtesy of Wally Motloch

What is particularly interesting about many – if not most – of these mega stone structures is that the individual stones cannot be moved or lifted by any existing modern technology, according to construction experts. The Anunnaki obviously did move and place them precisely, by some means yet to be replicated in modern times.[85]

The photos in Sitchin's two books describing his expeditions and travels show incontrovertible evidence that the mega stone structures discussed here do in fact have ancient origins. The Baalbek phenomena alone should remove all doubt that the Sitchin discussion of a space vehicle landing site is verifiable. Taken together with all the other evidence, the Sitchin paradigm can be confirmed as valid. These phenomena should – but probably still don't – silence the debunkers who criticize the Sitchin findings. But, it seems likely that no amount of physical evidence satisfies many of these skeptics who argue the facts that confirm the Anunnaki presence here on Earth. As Kuhn has reminded us, the old explanations die hard, and for some, explanations of long standing never can be rewritten in the minds of the old guard –

regardless of the visible and written evidence, which supports the new paradigm.

These phenomena pose the unanswered questions from the existing (normal science) explanatory framework. According to Kuhn, even a new paradigm leaves unanswered questions. However, the Sitchin paradigm is a powerful body of findings and explanations. In sum, the overarching impact of Sitchin's work supports the assertion that a new paradigm now is in place.

And finally, the Sitchin work has a future impact: it gives us the assurance that "we are not alone in the Universe" and Planet Nibiru will return.

CHAPTER THREE

THE SITCHIN ENCOUNTER EXPERIENCE

Bravery is shown by those with the clearest vision
of what is before them, glory and danger alike,
and not withstanding these,
go out to meet it.

—Dialogue by character, Leopold, Duke of Albany,
played by Hugh Jackman in the movie
Kate and Leopold.[86]

What readers of any of Zecharia Sitchin's books clearly realize is that Sitchin is a *brave* explorer. His explanations cut a wide swath across several "jungles" on the conceptual landscape, but it is we, the readers, who do the discovering on his expeditions. How do we know he is brave? Look at the evidence. He ventures into what most of us would call a "no man's land," consisting of ancient clay tablets scribed in an ancient cuneiform language, where his space- age mindset allows him to read and then reinterpret these texts. Then, having realized the inscribed stories on the ancient clay tablets originally were misinterpreted (because the original redactors were writing well before our space-age), he lays out his findings, confident they are supported by historical facts, artifacts, and written evidence. Finally, he reports in published form – as did the early explorers – to his armchair audience. This is the tradition of the early explorers, and what Sitchin has done.

It is an understatement to say that Zecharia Sitchin's work breaks new ground. Obviously he is a bold, daring, self-confident, and undaunted researcher. In 1976, his first book, *The 12ᵗʰ Planet*, written after years of linguistic, historical, and scientific study, tells the story of a small group of technologically advanced space travelers who first came to

Earth 445,000 years ago. The information he found when he studied for himself the ancient clay tablets supports this understanding. It did not, in Sitchin's mind, describe the mythical beliefs of the Sumerians, as the first scholars who studied these materials said, but instead, laid out information mostly *given* to the Sumarians by a small group of interplanetary travelers.

It becomes obvious to those who look seriously at Sitchin's work that the information presented in his several books, taken together, contains numerous far-reaching implications of such a profound nature that after a first encounter, even the skeptical reader is compelled to *deal in some way* with the content of his work.

Interestingly, Sitchin readers cannot passively glide through the pages of his carefully crafted discussions without realizing nearly every page contains new – and decisively unique – information. Having encountered even one of his publications, the reader is obliged to ask: What does one *do* with this new information? The next steps are clear. First-time readers must confront the fact that the substance of Sitchin's material lies outside and beyond their already developed understandings. These readers fast come to realize that the explanation of human origins that we have learned from physical anthropologists, at best, is incomplete, and probably is wrong. With the reading of each new chapter, we are enlightened and subtly and irreversibly moved into another way of understanding, forced to enter another reality, one ripe with implications for the way we make meaning about the world's early history and who we are as humans. We also know something else: while Sitchin's explorations cut a wide swath across several jungles on the conceptual landscape, it is *we* the readers who do the learning on his research expedition.

Furthermore, this new body of information is made credible by the fact it is scribed in clay on tablets thousands of years old, thus is tangible. And this other new reality is made available to us through the bravery of a very talented and courageous man – Zecharia Sitchin.

When encountering Sitchin's books, we must keep in mind that when he undertook the challenging tasks of studying and then re-interpreting the translations of the early redactors, he held the modern mindset we now *all* hold, one that stems from the fact we live in the age of space technology, an age saturated with "flying machines," rockets that can carry men to other planetary bodies – for now, the Moon – and where powerful telescopes can gather graphic information from deep space. In fact, from our base of space-age technological achievement, modern society now is planning to send humans to Mars.

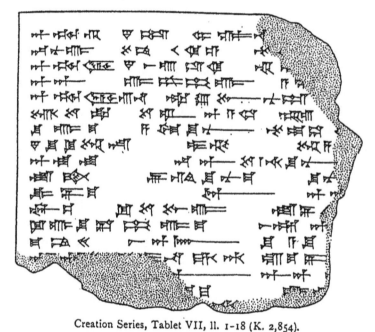

Creation Series, Tablet VII, ll. 1-18 (K. 2,854).

From the Epic of Creation, a supposed myth which tells of the creation of mankind for the service of the gods; a translation accepted by mainstrem scholars and expanded upon by Sitchin.

As one might expect, the re-interpretations presented by Sitchin are read with different levels of understanding by those who become curious about reports of his amazing message. A line that appears on the cover of Sitchin's first book, *The 12ᵗʰ Planet,* obviously intrigued the thousands who first looked at and even purchased this book. It says: *"Astonishing documentary evidence of Earth's celestial ancestors."*

Something else happens when the Sitchin's material is encountered. This information is rife with implications. These implications bring the reader face to face with his/her own personal frontier of knowledge. These implications suggest ideas we likely never have considered before. Moreover, these implications force us to consider the future – our personal future and that of the planet and its human inhabitants. To allow the Sitchin information into our accepted framework of explanation is to take a risk; this information threatens to enlarge our world view and also forces us to define our existing beliefs.

It is the structure and strength of our personal world view that is brought into question by his material. In fact, we are forced to confront our *world view* in an "up close and personal" way when we encounter Sitchin's information because his explanations shake up – even attack – everything we previously have learned. We find that our world view must be scrutinized because it informs our ability to think critically and analytically about any body of information. It is our existing world view that determines whether we can – or will – accept new information. It is our world view that determines our beliefs, and defines which ideas we will let in, and which ones we will keep out. If we lean toward acceptance of the Sitchin material, we must release our conceptual hold on what we previously came to believe to be true, accepting in its place the Sitchin explanations. On the other hand, if we find our thoughts taking a rejecting stance, then likely doubt, distrust, uncertainty and a sense of being personally attacked may permeate our thinking.

To tinker with our world view is dangerous. Our personal world view organizes and constructs who we are, thereby giving shape and boundary to what we are willing – and able – to see and learn about the world. To accept new, previously unheard of information – especially provocative information – means we need to re-organize *all* that material already in place, and that is a *huge* undertaking. It doesn't take much reflective thought to realize the scope of the rethinking and readjustment one needs to do.

The Acceptance Psychology

When we analyze how we "felt" after first reading the Sitchin material, we come face to face with an array of emotions. Certainly we were perplexed and even bewildered. In fact, our initial thoughts probably were tinged with doubt, hesitancy, skepticism, and even initial disbelief. Our emotional responses color our intellectual capability. Some of us found an intuitive understanding and acceptance of this provocative material. Regardless, we had to decide whether what we were reading was true – or not. We first had to remind ourselves that what we were encountering was a completely different explanation than we had ever heard of or encountered before. If we stayed with this emerging awareness and read further, what we began to realize was that a *shift* in our way of making meaning was in motion. Then, our thoughts began to "toggle back and forth" between such considerations as "Wow, this is stuff seems fantastic! But, wait a minute, it can't be true – can it? But look at the evidence this guy brings forward. Wow! Maybe it all is true. If it is true, what does it all mean?"

In fact, if we were giving serious thought to the validity of Sitchin's information, it is likely that our entire way of thinking was enlarging under this set of thoughts. Acknowledging this array of considerations indicates we were, in actuality, "processing" in a positive way the impact of our Sitchin encounter. Likely this took a bit of time, though after we recovered from this mind-blowing awareness, the implications for our "old" way of making meaning became clear. We realized that we needed to alter, or more likely abandon, the original things we learned and replace them with this new information. In other words, we had to rebuild our world view by creating a new larger place in our reservoir of learned information within which to lodge this new way of making meaning. To do this, we needed to weed out the old way of thinking and replace it with the new.

Cataloging all the types of knowledge that needed adjusting, and redefining the linkages between this new information and our old beliefs, ideas, and perspectives constituted the intellectual work we needed to undertake, *if* we came through the Sitchin encounter with an accepting conclusion. Those who did this intellectual work can be applauded for their willingness to undertake these far-reaching intellectual tasks.

The Rejection Psychology

Several possible reasons account for one who encounters Sitchin's work and develops a *rejecting* stance. Such a decision, while seemingly informed by commonsense, is prompted by an emotional dimension that emerges during the first encounter. At the outset of the encounter, a self-protective "knee jerk" response flares up, and almost without a second thought, the information is rejected. Likely it is a feeling of being threatened by the material that arises. Rejection suggests that one experiences a sudden, unconscious realization, one based on the awareness that one's personal world view is either wrong or outdated; certainly this world view must be inadequate *if* the Sitchin information holds any validity.

Those who readily rejected the Sitchin information (assuming they even gave it cursory consideration) can bring forward a plethora of reasons why the Sitchin information cannot be given further consideration. The cascading thoughts that likely characterize this emotional reaction are like this: "This information must be completely wrong. I have never heard of anything like it before. Who is this guy? He's not an expert that I have ever heard of. Where did he get this material? Who is he to put forward this stuff?"

Let's look more deeply into this negative reaction. What is attacked in this type of reaction is one's world view. All the effort that went into learning how to see and explain the world likely is now under threat, and its validity is called into question by Sitchin's far-reaching discussion. A world view gives us a sense of security. It operates like our attitudes, clinging in an almost unrecognizable way to the deeper constructs in our reservoir of opinion and knowledge. In these deep spaces, we also store our values and beliefs. All this "stuff" is what we call *our knowledge*. Our individual world view is the container for all these beliefs, opinions, and other closely-held structures – like values. Typically we strengthened the walls of our world view through tedious intellectual work, and like any protective structure, our world view represents something we can retreat into when the "winds of threat" blow hard. In other words, our world view is our base of security.

When we look closely at what props up our world view, we find, in actuality, it is our *sense of self*. New perspectives and new information must be integrated into our existing explanation of who we believe we are, requiring a reconstruction – or at least an enlarging of – our self-concept. Our sense of self defines the inner dimensions and meanings we hold about our identity. Because our self concept organizes and constructs our reality, the implication here is clear: when we encounter provocative new information we have to first sort it, and then evaluate it, and then try to integrate it into our self concept. The larger and more tightly held our self concept is, the more difficult it is to even think about allowing new information into it, to say nothing about accepting it. In reality, rejecting new provocative information is easier to do than is accepting it.

So, when one's world view is challenged by information that takes one beyond their accumulated experience and knowledge, some individuals fight back with a strong *denial reaction*. They deny both the validity of the information that generates the threat, and they strive to devalue any possible importance this "new stuff" carries. Assuming an attack mode allows one to feel superior, in control, and relieves any sense of insecurity. Those who are captured under this type of reaction find themselves thinking, "No, no, no. It isn't like that. I know this stuff is wrong. My accumulated knowledge and expertise are in jeopardy if I even seriously consider – let alone accept – this stuff. I'll have to completely abandon what I have learned. I'll have to admit that what I have built as my expertise and base of knowledge was incomplete, and perhaps even wrong. I'll have to let go of the way I think about many of the things I have come to value." Rejection leaves the individual with this decision: "I can't do all that. I won't do all that."

If we consider ourselves even fairly well-educated, or more importantly, if our personal expertise is called into question by this new material, and if the implications of Sitchin's material would overturn our established base of knowledge, we are forced to face a serious threat to our ego. When these types of questions arise, clearly it is the ego's voice (comprised of the persistence of the words *I, I, I,* and *me, my* and *mine)* that has stepped forward and clearly signals its command over any judgments to be made. Every thought – and emotion – that informs such a negative reaction now is under the self-protective control of the ego. The ego clearly aims to defend its controlling power by first attacking the validity of the information, and then it turns full force on the author of the new material. Typically what happens is that the author of this new provocative information is accused of being a "fraud," or worse, he is called a "*heretic.*"[87]

The public at large seems to have less trouble engaging Sitchin's material in a positive way than does most of the community of academics and scholars that encounters it. Supposedly, we academics and scientists are committed to advancing the boundaries of knowledge. This is the ultimate purpose of all scientific inquiry. All too often, attention to advancing the frontiers of knowledge is only a "lip

photo by Paul Tice

service" objective. For far too many academics it is the ego that is in control of one's opinions. Reputation is all important in the academic arena. One's expounded expertise is the way one's reputation is made and the way it survives to identify a credible thinker and scholar. It cannot be compromised by being drawn into accepting a potentially unsound body of information that may be proven wrong in the future.

There is little that can be done with those whose accumulated expertise is attacked and forces them to reject the Sitchin information. Rational and persuasive argument with these individuals is futile because logic is not the ground on which "irrational" battles are fought. When emotion is at the root of rejection, little can be done by means of rational argument. It is only the intellectually brave and open minded among this group who will give serious consideration to Sitchin's contribution. Some skeptics will wait until the new explanatory paradigm is so well established that they have little ground left on which to attach their denial. Others, according to Thomas Kuhn, *never will* accept new information that seemingly contradicts their original understandings and explanations. [88] The old guard will need to die out, holding tight to their denial. What is required is a new generation who, with fresh and open minds, can give due consideration to a new paradigm.

CHAPTER FOUR

THE IMPACT OF THE SHIFTED PARADIGM

A life is not important except in the impact it has on other lives.

—Epitaph written by
Jackie Robinson

Once the mind is expanded it cannot go back to its original size.

—Oliver Wendell Holmes

As social beings, we do not live outside that body of explanations that we have learned to depend upon. These explanations comprise what Thomas Kuhn calls normal science. It encompasses what we know about the world. In fact, we were raised with these explanations.[89] These are the ways we learned to make meaning, and the ways that guided all of our learning trajectories. According to Hans Mohr, a practicing scientist whose work is strongly philosophical, [90] we learn that operating paradigms (normal science) include a definite line of thinking – the acceptable trajectory of cultural thought. They shape what we believe to be "the way it is," and this operates for scientist and layman alike. Mohr goes further. He confesses that anyone making even a minor step outside the existing paradigm can encounter "… strong and embittered reluctance."[91]

Allegedly, new ideas are encouraged in the realm of normal science. We are taught that the role of science (as a field of study) is to question existing paradigms, to test the theories that these frameworks encompass, to construct new models, and, with reputable evidence and accurately collected and interpreted data, to evaluate the explanatory power of the existing paradigms. When a *new* paradigm emerges, it is the role of science to evaluate its capacity for explanation, and to determine if the new framework is more complete, richer, and contains a wider scope of explanations. However, in spite of what the history of new, provocative ideas and research findings has shown, the really superior and provocative new ideas, more often than not, are treated disdainfully when first set out.

Making serious changes in our intellectual habits of thinking is a rare event. Seldom have we had to even think about doing these sorts of mental tasks. However, dealing with a shifted paradigm is not a new experience in the history of scientific thought. John L. Casti, a highly acclaimed mathematician and philosopher of science, characterizes our way of approaching new material like this: we start by making meaning and interpreting information by using a pair of conceptual glasses through which we typically see and engage the world in order to solve its puzzles – those that arise in the familiar realm of normal science. Suddenly, when confronted with the new paradigm, our glasses are smashed. When we put on a new pair, what (and how) we see is quite different. This new view is the *impact of the shifted paradigm*.[92]

Mounting any challenge to the *status quo* holds potential for weakening the existing operational ways of thinking. Observations and explanations that previously appeared to "fit" under the old frameworks no longer do. The old explanations become inadequate, or even can begin to be considered to be incorrect. The old explanatory frameworks are in serious trouble when an ever-increasing body of old observations are considered to be questionable. The tide begins to turn when the sharp, open-minded thinkers among us suddenly become converts to the new explanations. Almost immediately, these converts seem to lose their confidence in the old traditional way of making meaning that was part of the previous framework of explanations, especially after these brave thinkers see the enlarged scope of the new explanations. These converts recognize that an enlarged scope of explanation is available for consideration, one that holds far-reaching implications not even visible previously.

The New Shifted Paradigm

Now let us look carefully at the types of things that happen when a paradigm shifts. When the shift begins, at first no order exists – only chaos reigns. When this kind of an upheaval is initiated, according to John Casti, *everything* related to the old construct must be re-examined and most likely needs to be transformed.[93] In the beginning, logic typically has little to do with seeing and accepting the new paradigm. Clearly, the revolution is on its way when a "gestalt switch" or a "conversion" occurs in the way of thinking of a group of converts. In the beginning, only a small group seriously engages the new material. A bond grows up between the members of this group because these individuals share a similar way of conceptualizing and understanding the world. Typically this group of converts to the new paradigm enlarges as time goes on. It may take years for it to grow to a substantial size.

As members of society, we appreciate and respect the old way of explaining ideas, events, processes, and consequences that we have come to understand as valid. This body of traditional explanation illuminates our accumulated knowledge of the material, biological, technological, and scientific worlds. This information has been carefully taught and learned by us over our lifetimes. These ways of thinking represent an enormous body of hard-won knowledge that is acquired through considerable personal sacrifice. In fact, this is why we think long and hard before "grabbing" onto a very different body of new explanations.

If it is extremely difficult to let go of old ways of thinking, how do new ideas, grounded provable ideas, those that coalesce the largest array of facts and recast old explanations into a more comprehensive model, *ideas that shift the paradigm*, ever get to see the light of day? And, when they do catch on, how do they survive? The answer is clear: the author of such bold and overarching ideas must be factually confident and personally steadfast in his belief that the new way of thinking is more than interesting; he must believe it to be *beneficial to humanity*. If we need to assign an overarching motivation to Sitchin's work, beyond that of bringing provable ancient evidence into our modern mindset, it is that the events of ancient history will have serious consequences for Earth's inhabitants *in the future*.

The supporters of this new way of making meaning – the new paradigm – must assist in carrying forward the seemingly controversial new message. Sitchin's proponents must persevere in "taking it on the chin" when detractors and debunkers make negative comments and launch attacks – even when these critics launch accusations about the gullibility of anyone who would accept such "outlandish" material. What the proponents must do, symbolically speaking, is to put reconstituted new wine into completely different bottles and re-label it. But, obviously, the proponents of the shifted paradigm can not force the deniers and debunkers to drink it.

The Sitchin Impact

For those who intuitively and intellectually accepted Sitchin's explanations in their initial encounter, coming up with an explanation of how this occurred – or even why they accepted it – is nearly impossible. Their acceptance of the Sitchin paradigm integrated into their thinking effortlessly. The impact of Sitchin's logic just seemed to "resonate" within their self-concept. These "converts" often found themselves wanting to paraphrase the enlightening ideas and explanations they read in Sitchin's books in order to share this information with friends. Often, they give copies of one – or more – of Sitchin's books to friends in hopes that others will see the logic of the Sitchin information, and thereby share their own excitement and sense of discovery.

As a result of the insidious impact of the Sitchin findings, a major change of perspective does indeed take place in the minds of those who accept his new ideas. His work pushes all of the contemporary (old) explanations back into the normal science category of explanation and frees us to see beyond our personal frontiers of knowledge. Sitchin's careful, scholarly re-interpretation of the ancient evidence catapults us into an "other world" where we find ourselves lonely among our colleagues. In short, Sitchin has generated what Thomas Kuhn has called a *scientific revolution.*

On the other hand, for those who come through the Sitchin encounter with a negative reaction, there is almost nothing that can be said to change this reaction. Attempts to "convince" an individual who holds entrenched beliefs that prevent him or her from accepting Sitchin's material and to change those old views usually are futile. The non-accepting reaction of these individuals is tightly wrapped in a very personal set of emotions. An argument requires two people who simultaneously hold logical and rational capabilities, and a "denier" is one who behaves through a screen of emotions. We must remind ourselves that developing new ways of thinking is not easy. The need for adjustment to the new mindset falls only on those who are sufficiently open-minded enough – and mentally agile enough – to see the logic and coherence of Sitchin's explanations. Around the world, the "acceptors" now include thousands who have read Sitchin books. If anyone needs supportive facts to bolster their own mindset, the size of the avalanche of "acceptors" should do it.

If we pause for a moment to ask: How did Sitchin's books come to catch on? They sell by the thousands. These books hold their own in the publishing arena because his discussion covers new ground by providing the evidence to fuel new ways of thinking. Sitchin's discussions capture the "explorer" mindset that many new age thinkers hold. Most importantly, his books are extremely well written, and contain a plethora of documented evidence so that accepting readers are captivated by the trajectory of new learning that his discussions put in motion. Publishers around the world see this potential impact on audiences and do not hesitate to enlist translators to make the Sitchin message available in their own language. [94]

Negative assaults are another type of impact of the Sitchin paradigm. One can only wonder specifically how he dealt with criticism. He tolerated criticism by ignoring it. However, when one got close enough to him to learn about his strength of character and the single-mindedness that shaped his research (and his personality), one can see that these qualities fueled his unswerving confidence in the correctness of his research. Sitchin humbly wore this self-assurance as a shielding armor. He also held another strength. He clearly understood that criticism was inevitable, but he did not engage it. Few of us have the toughness and strength of character to withstand criticism, especially that which attacks our intellect and our creative work, but Sitchen did. He did not suffer fools easily, but he also did not engage them. He also did not attempt to "sell" his findings, but instead set out to teach people who came to hear his presentations about it. For anyone who did not resonate with his explanations, it was their loss.

Sitchin was an enormously curious person, and he was doggedly persistent in following up on unanswered details. Once he began to see coherence in the tablet stories, when they were viewed as *actual* history, he did not let go. Instead he pursued the enigmatic parts until he figured out an entire logical explanation. He realized that the early scholars did not have the benefit of the space-age perspectives that he – and all of us – now hold. As he enlarged his personal base of scientific knowledge to render explanations of the puzzling "bits and snips" held in "coded" form in the ancient material, his determination to figure out the whole meaning energized him. Like working on a picture puzzle, he kept finding pieces that "fit." Each interpretive success served as stimulus that energized him to go even further into source material.

Let us consider the impact of one of the most provocative topics included in the Sitchin work: the origins of homo sapiens.

When we look at the well-worn explanations of human origins, we find two of these explanations form a raging debate. Each takes an almost irreconcilable position against the other. Here we will call these discussions the *human origins debate.* In this debate, human *evolution,* as given by the traditional scientific explanations, is pitted against the religiously structured argument, one that stems from a literal reading of the *Bible*, particularly the Book of *Genesis.* This side of the debate is known under the label of *creationism.*

It is not our intent here to delve into either of the debate positions in detail, or to take one side or the other. We only will point out that this debate continues with each side claiming to hold the true explanation.

Enki and Ninharsag modifying or "creating" mankind.

When we draw on the exegesis on human origins provided by Sitchin, what we find is a highly provocative message indeed. If we were reading science fiction, we could dismiss Sitchin's findings. However, his explanation is well-reasoned, rational, and factually grounded, based on the tangible evidence from the clay tablets. This evidence comes in the form of a cylinder seal, an image carved in reverse, then rolled onto clay. It creates a pictorial image showing two beings ("gods"). The figure on the left stands in front of a rack of test tubes, while the one on the right (a female) is holding up a small being. The accompanying text to this clay tablet depiction says (from the female): "Look what my hands have wrought." It is clear from this depiction and its accompanying text that some unconventional-looking beings were successfully involved in some sort of scientific endeavor. Using the Sitchin information, derived as it is from the tablets, we learn that the figures represent the Anunnaki Enki and his sister, Ninharsag, who came to Earth as Chief Medical Officer. She and Enki performed the genetic engineering tasks.[95] Further evidence from the tablets tells us that, after numerous attempts that failed, the successful combination was achieved with genetic material taken from an Anunnaki male and from a female hominid found to already live on Earth. This combination proved to bring forward a blended genetic combination that established a "creative" miracle – humans.

So, instead of the existing (uninformed) either-or debate, what the Sitchin material tells us is that a "new" explanation put forward in the Sumerian tablet materials *enriches* the origins debate. This alternative explanation for human origins rightfully can be called the "other terrestrial origins" explanation. Instead of an "either-or" debate, we have an explanation that contains *both sides* of the original debate. The Anunnaki ("gods") "created" the human species by using their own genes, mixed with those of a hominid that was the product of evolution.[96]

Taking this explanation into account, we can look back at the two positions in the debate and see that both have a bit of legitimacy. Whereas the female hominid was a product of evolution, the Anunnaki genes combined to produce a specimen that was indeed a "creation."[97] Suffice it to say that the tablets were scribed three millennia *before* the *Bible,* and the *Bible* condenses the much older Sumerian stories. Sitchin points out that the tablets illuminate the stories in the Book of *Genesis* that are the source for the creationist position. The important point here goes beyond how the tablets inform the Bible, but that a *new* interpretation comes forward to offer a different way of referring to the origins debate. In reality, this constitutes a *both-and* explanation.

With the growing popularity of Sitchin's reputation, and publication of his several newer books, a variety of criticism has come forward that attacks the validity of his work. However, most of these criticisms are devoid of a thorough examination of his sources and careful examination of the archaeological evidence that proves his conclusions to be accurate.

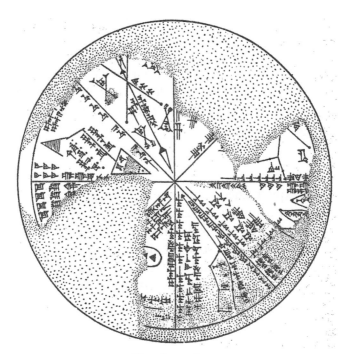

The planesphere

One such piece of evidence depicts how the Anunnaki maneuvered their spacecraft through the solar system's outer planets on their approach to Earth. Found in the ruins of the Royal Library in Nineveh, this artifact now is part of the British Museum's collection. I saw this object for myself, with Sitchin, during a visit there. It takes the form of a planesphere (the reproduction of a spherical surface on a flat map).[98] This object was identified, by experts from the British Royal Astronomical Society,[99] to contain cuneiform signs that are excellently preserved. While the object itself is irregularly damaged, it's undamaged portions show symbols recounting space navigational information used by the Anunnaki leader Enlil to navigate through the outer planets of our solar system. The information on this artifact was first analyzed by Ernst Weidner, a German scholar, and published in his major textbook, *Handbuch der Babylonischen Astronomie* (1915). In his attempts to analyze the tablet, Weidner concluded that it did not make sense. Sitchin takes on this interpretive task and publishes his analysis:

...there can hardly be any doubt that the tablet (using the Sumerian meaning of the [repeating] word-syllables ...is a route map, marking the way by which the god Enlil went by the [outer] planets.... Descending from a point which is "high high high high," through vapor clouds and a lower zone that was... vaporless, toward the horizon point, where the skies and the ground meet.[100]

This is an example of how Sitchin's extensive knowledge bore fruit. He was able to explain successfully what other scholars, who worked hard but could not decipher the ancient texts, could not. They were without the wisdom contained in Sitchin's full body of interpretive work. When the other early scholars did their analyses and writings, they still assumed that the tablets were discussing ethereal beings that the Sumerians believed to be supernatural. Remember, Sitchin's understanding of the Anunnaki ability to traverse space gave him the ability to understand how Enlil came to be flying through the outer solar system.

What is significant is that Sitchin's expertise deciphered this and thousands of other tangible artifacts on display in museums around the world. All this re-interpreted evidence testifies to the validity of Anunnaki presence on Earth, and their ability to traverse between their planet, Nibiru, and Earth. This body of understandings combines to give the Sitchin paradigm its strength and validity.

Now we pose some important questions: After the paradigm shifts, then what? What are the implications for the future of this different, provocative, well supported body of explanation that greatly enlarges our understanding of ancient history? Certainly the implications for the future need to be given serious attention. But, how do we do that? How can we even begin to discuss future impacts rationally and scientifically? Having looked seriously into the field of future studies, we will draw on a methodology used by futures analysts, and apply it to the Sitchin paradigm. Our discussion now turns to unfolding this methodology, and then using it to answer questions generated by Sitchin's work. What comes next? What does the future hold?

CHAPTER FIVE

THE FUTURE IMPLICATIONS OF
SITCHIN'S CONTRIBUTION

If you have the ability to change the world,
you have the responsibility to do so.
If you don't, who will?

Anyone can visualize a future.
Not many know how to get there.

We first imagine our future.
After that, we live it.

—From John L. Petersen's book
A Vision for 2012: Planning for
Extraordinary Change[101]

After the paradigm shifts – then what? What are the future
implications of Sitchin's findings and explanations that will unfold
as we move forward in time?[102] Certainly future implications need to
be identified and explored so we can begin to plan for positive – and
negative – impacts. But, how do we do that? We can not see into the
future, so how can we even begin to discuss future impacts?

Future-oriented questions are not new queries for the practitioners
and students of future studies, a field of study that has an identifiable
methodology and has generated considerable scholarship. Two futurist
educators, Robert Fitch and Cordell Svengalis, indicate that studying
the future is an idea often referred to but seldom given serious attention.
To study how to "think forward in time" is an easily developed skill –
provided one is not bogged down in retro-thinking – otherwise known

as "Monday-morning quarterbacking." The purpose of futures study (futurism) focuses on giving us the tools to develop understandings, attitudes, and abilities, which can assist us to deal effectively with change.[103]

In actuality, conceptualizing future scenarios is an extension of our almost intuitive future-oriented thought processes. Any time we plan a trip, think about a new job, anticipate an upcoming birthday or holiday, we are projecting out on the time line that moves in a linear manner to that realm we have come to conceptualize as the "near future." In the professional world of futurizing, this typically covers a 5 to 50 span of years. In our personal world, it begins tomorrow.

To implement this future thinking mindset, one must *not* be burdened by a fear that any conjectures set out, or future scenarios designed, will prove to be wrong. Successful future thinking beyond the five year horizon requires a brave, bold thinker.[104] It is only the near future that we will focus on here, because of the multitude of unexpected phenomena that can "pop up" to force alterations in any trajectory that may be in motion or projected. These unexpected phenomena are what John L. Petersen, an accomplished futurist, calls "wild cards." [105]

A distinguished futurist and founder of the World Future Society, Edwin Cornish, indicates that futurists have a unique perspective on the world. In his view, a futures perspective consists of and builds on three underlying assumptions. The first is that futurists assume that a *unity of reality* exists, and this unity is interconnected across time. You can't "time warp" into a viable future. Just as jets move progressively through space, we move in a linear and connected way through time. Second, futurists assume that workable "chunks" of time, a fourth dimension variable, are crucial factors for estimating and establishing goals. Planners look at a future time horizon and assess how much time (and money) will be consumed by each step in order to reach a projected future date. Deadlines are the anticipation of projections that can be reached with steady progress along a linear time line. In our society we have considerable expertise in "managing" the near future by this type of goal-setting. Third, futurists assume that ideas (thoughts, conjectures) focused on the future form the basis of reasonable projections. Ideas are considered *futurables*, in the commodity sense, and are the "tools of thought" of the futures tradition.[106] However, thinking in a futures mode is a legitimate activity, and is a method of rationally projected conceptualizing.[107] It is not prediction.

The Futures Methodology

Using a futures perspective for analysis forces us to look at information already known in order to identify *trends in motion*. These likely outcomes serve to open consideration to more likely outcomes, and thus can be organized under a four-part model that allows an approach to conceptualizing future outcomes. The four types of outcomes are future situations or events that are **possible, probable, preferable,** and **plausible** futures. These four ways of projecting outcomes comprise the framework of analysis set out by futurist Norman Henchy.[108] *Possible* futures consist of *what may be*; *probable* considers *what will likely be*; *preferable* futures deal with *what should be*; and *plausible* futures give attention *to what could be*.

Before we focus on the future implications of Sitchin's work, as a way to illustrate how this futures methodology works, we will look again at the argument we previously introduced called the "origins debate" (see Chapter 4). This debate is well-known under the pre-Sitchin normal science perspective. We can subject the structure of this debate, the two original positions – evolutionist and creationist – to a futures analysis to demonstrate how the four futures dimensions can be employed. Keep in mind: *Possible outcomes* look at the logically connected options that extend trends already in motion. Some qualities of viable possible outcome choices include those that are enlightening, satisfying, constructive, beneficial, educational, palatable, tolerable, or even disdainful. *Probable outcomes* allow us to consider each identified possible outcome in terms of the mathematical probability of its success. Of course, probable outcomes also can be considered to be based on the strength of existing evidence. *Preferable outcomes* give us permission to weave in personal and societal values. This option brings into play personal free-will choice and allows us also to consider its role and influence in making a selection of outcomes we are willing and able to accept. This is akin to making the selection of which path we would *like to* walk to get to a destination, and selecting the one that would allow us to see the type of scenery we value most. We also would hold in consideration the amount of expense (in time and money) we are willing and able to accept. Preferable outcomes typically have a pay-off. And finally, *plausible outcomes* allow us to consider what *could be*. These outcomes open the range of future considerations to encompass strategic, financially feasible, politically viable, as well as likely ecological and human resource outcomes.

The Future of the Origins Debate: An Illustrative Example

Re-examining the origins debate under a futures methodology, we can consider one *possible* future outcome to be that both evolutionists and creationists hold firm to their current contentious positions, thus maintaining the "status quo" (possible future 1). Another option open for consideration is that one side in this seemingly intractable debate – either one – will acknowledge the enlarged viewpoint set out by the Sitchin paradigm, and the debate will shift its focus to consider ancient evidence (possible future 2). The third possible outcome is that both sides will "shift" to acknowledge the logic and wisdom that is inherent in the Sitchin position, thereby redefining discussion – perhaps as previously suggested, calling it the "other terrestrial genetic manipulation" discussion (possible future 3).

Looking at *probable future outcomes* of this debate requires us to assess the mathematical probability of each of the range of possibilities. Using a mathematical approach, three possibilities exist (as outlined above). A probability of one-third ($p = 0.333$) can be assigned to each possible outcome. The decimal number assigned here follows probability analysis in which it is assumed that each possibility has an *equal* chance of selection (when each probability is added together, it must equal an integer, $p = 1.0$).

However, because of the underlying assumption of the interconnectedness of reality, we must acknowledge the contextual (societal) circumstances in which these possibilities are posited. Confounding factors impinge on our ability to work with confidence with equal probabilities. In the origins debate, each side believes in their definition of rationality and the immutability of their position. We must consider the nature and source of the evidence used by each side in this debate that is under consideration. Faith is at the root of one position, underpinned by a literal belief that the *Bible's* book of *Genesis* is true. Scientifically based factual evidence, on the other hand, underpins the evolutionary position, but this position also has a context built into it by the evidence (and associated conclusions drawn about it) by the disciplines that form the accepted sciences dealing with human origins. These include (but are limited to) physical anthropology, genetics, and paleo-anthropology.

When examined closely, the two opposing sides of the human origins argument cannot be reconciled on the basis of their supporting bodies of evidence. Faith is emotionally defined (meaning it tends to disregard rational argument), and leads to full rejection of the other side's evidence. Factual evidence is held as important to the scientific side, provided that it is selected and analyzed under the terms of the scientific method, and the application of these methods of analysis employs and maintains accuracy and objectivity.

Are there any other possible futures for the origins debate? Yes. Another possible future is indicated in the work of Thomas Kuhn. He tells us that existing (normal science) paradigms eventually must "die out," primarily because those who hold the disbelieving position never will change. They are eliminated through time – essentially they age out. When the Sitchin paradigm becomes a viable body of information and is widely infused into mainstream culture, it 'will inform new considerations that support the newly proposed "other terrestrial origins" explanation. The young, with their fresh receptive minds, will process and accept the new Sitchin paradigm perspectives, provided they are allowed to be exposed to them.   If this happens, a new body of considerations would inform each side of the debate.

In this origins debate, another confounding but important factor must be brought into the discussion. The second and third possible future outcomes (suggested above) bring Sitchin's contribution into the scenario. Within both constituencies (the literalist religious arena and the scientific arena) there are those who won't even consider and therefore do not accept Sitchin's work at this time. So, while we bring this new Sitchin perspective into the possible scenarios we consider, it is unrealistic to assume more than a fifty-percent probability of acceptance (p. = 0.50) within each of these constituencies. The percentage of each side who accept the Sitchin paradigm needs to be ascertained. Only then can accurate probabilities be assigned, and a sequential trajectory of probabilities be run.

Let us now turn to *preferable* futures. Under this type of futures consideration, individual personal choices enter the process of defining outcomes. Each of us must define the preferable outcomes that illuminate our own values. If this writer were the "designer" of the preferable future options for the origins debate, elimination of this debate altogether would be the preferable option. This could be accomplished by disseminating a wide array of evidence that would overturn and reorganize the literalist interpretation of the *Bible*. This could be accomplished by making widely available the interpreted ancient Sumerian texts that, incidentally, show them to be the sources from which the writers of *Genesis* drew. Additionally, works from the *Pseudepigrapha*,[109] the texts extant at the time of the debates over what information was to be included in the *Bible*, would again be widely disseminated. Much of this material illuminates and perhaps even redefines what has come to be called "biblical wisdom." By widening the availability of ancient manuscripts − and giving them legitimacy − the public could develop different considerations, and new insights likely would develop. The *Bible* has held sway as almost the only widely available textual basis for faith for some 1500 years for Christians, and double that length of time for Jews. The Koran, the volume guiding belief and behavior for Muslim adherents, has influenced that faith for just over 1300 years. Perhaps it is time in the history of humankind to reconsider the limited array of textual materials that inform religious belief structures, and put forward serious efforts to enlarge the arena of information used to inform faith and belief in the future societies of the world.

The final dimension of the futures methodology is *plausible* futures – *what could be*. This dimension of the futures methodology brings to bear a wide array of philosophical and scientific approaches. Scenarios set out under this dimension should be drawn from a range of fields of study, such as systems theory, economics, systematic philosophy, ecology, policy studies, and management sciences.[110] This debate has no relevance to future ecological or economic outcomes. In the context in which the origins debate is promulgated, few of these fields seem relevant.

Future Implication of The Return of Nibiru and the Anunnaki

Over the years following the publication of his first book, Sitchin gave a wide variety of presentations and spoke to numerous conference audiences. At the end of his presentations, he often opened the floor to audience questions. Perhaps the most pervasive question that came forward was **"When will the Anunnaki return?"** With the skill of a magician who deftly sidesteps questions asking how he performed his illusions, Sitchin managed to do likewise. While he wanted to be forthright, probably having ascertained a likely answer during his research efforts, Sitchin *never offered a date* – until now. He indicated on several occasions that *if* he gave a specific date, and it was found to be wrong, skepticism and incredulity might infect other aspects of his findings. Offering an exact date would leave room for pundits to criticize all of his findings. This is because, according to Sitchin, the return cannot be scientifically predicted. It contains a "margin of error" in the magnitude of 100 to 300 years because of the enormity of that planet's orbit.

Having offered this caveat, Sitchin does consider evidence that may alter the potential uncertainty of the return. In 2007 Sitchin published his eleventh book titled *The End of Days: Armageddon and Prophecies of the Return*. This volume presents the evidence from the tablets indicating that the Past *is* the Future – and that humankind and planet Earth are subject to a predetermined cycle called "Celestial Time."[111] This book draws together historical and biblical evidence that shows the scope of the similarities between the current twenty-first century and the twenty-first century B.C.E. These similarities, Sitchin believes, are the "signal" of a return of Nibiru during *this century*. In this book's Preface, Sitchin gives a list of six future-oriented questions, indicating that they express people's deepest hopes and anxieties, and he goes on to state that they are "…questions that I dared not answer all these years – but now are questions the answers to which cannot – *must not* – be delayed."[112] *This strident statement is prophetic.*

Sitchin's *The End of Days* book details a plethora of information important to supporting his veiled prediction. One "nugget" embedded in this book deals with the NASA search during the 1980s for heat-emitting celestial bodies.   The probe was called the Infra-Red Astronomical Satellite. This project was assigned the mission to scan the edges of the solar system to gather all infra-red data. These data would include evidence of another planet coming in from deep space. This satellite *did* find a large object, recorded the signal, and checked it again six months later. The sensed object (still well beyond visual range) had *moved* in the direction of Earth. This first confirmation of Planet X, the name used by modern space scientists and astronomers, prompted the government to respond in ways similar to that which characterizes their response to UFO sightings. Following the press announcement of this observation, a governmental denial of the validity of the news report came forward. The day following the news of this event, it was announced that this finding was a "misunderstanding."

Yet this event, along with the Phobos incidents (discussed above), generated sufficient government concern to produce a set of government-issued guidelines called the *Declaration of Principles Concerning Activities Following the Detection of Extraterrestrial Intelligence.*[113] By its very existence, this document lends credence to the finding of Planet X, and perhaps knowledge of Sitchin's work. In fact, another extraordinary impact occurred on September 21, 1987 when President Regan addressed the United Nations, indicating that differences between nations likely would evaporate if Earth were confronted with the reality of aliens coming to this planet.

Sumerian cylinder seal imprint, circa 2500 B.C.

As to the *actual* date of the return, Sitchin draws on an inportant clay tablet image (made from a cylinder seal) that he depicts on the cover of *Of Heaven and Earth* and on page 260 in *The End of Days* book.[114] This image shows "...an astronaut on Mars (the sixth planet) communicating with one on Earth (the seventh planet, counting from the outside in) with a spacecraft in the heavens between them."[115] And the answer to the question of *when* these space travelers will return is shown on that tablet display *in the form of two intertwined fishes,* seen at the bottom-middle of the ancient depiction. This represents, to Sitchin, "...**a date inferred by its two fish symbol which refers to** *the Age of Pisces* (emphasis given in the original source)."[116] According to astrological sources, we now are approaching the end of the Age of Pisces and await the coming of the Age of Aquarius.[117] This would strongly suggest that the time of Nibiru's return is *in the near future.* As pointed out (above), prediction is not a feature of the futures methodology, so this discussion will "walk away" from the task of naming a specific date for the return – as did Sitchin.[118]

In an interview with a now disbanded publication, Sitchin made a point about an incorrect inference often made by his followers who read his first book. He said:

> ...as I have tried to explain in my recent seminars... the [Anunnaki] visits to Earth and the nearing (of what is called perihelion) of Nibiru do NOT coincide. This is a point of immense significance which those who have only read my first book somehow ignore.[119]

Based on this statement, likely, we can expect the Anunnaki to "visit" Earth both before and after Nibiru's passage around the Sun. This statement leaves us with an extremely provocative near future expectation. Another important understanding must be pointed out here. When Nibiru is sighted by our telescopic technology, the Anunnaki will likely already have returned to this planet!

Sitchin next to stone monument at Aleppo, Syria, which shows two winged figures, possibly gods, pointing to a planet.   photo courtesy of Wally Motloch

Possible Planetary Impacts

Several planetary impacts are associated with previous returns of Nibiru to the vicinity of Earth and while traveling through our solar system. It is useful to review some important historical evidence about the impact of previous returns of Nibiru that illuminate possible planetary impacts. According to the Creation tablets, Marduk (the huge invader planet) is responsible for Earth's current position, third from the Sun, after one of his moons inflicted a mighty blow on Tiamat (Earth's name when the planet orbited between Mars and Jupiter). If one of Marduk's several moons caused previous damage, as the *Enuma Elish* indicates, the *possibility* exists that an impact from one of his moons *may happen again.*

Statuette of Sumerian King Itur-Samagan of Mari, circa 2500 B.C., a possible Anunnaki god who could return with Nibiru.

photo courtesy of Gaye and Sergio Lub

The historical material tells of other serious impacts that occurred when Nibiru returned. Tablet evidence indicates that tectonic activity is provoked by planet Nibiru, a body estimated to be 3 to 5 times larger than Earth. This planet's proximity would cause considerable gravitational effects and electromagnetic reactions effecting Earth's most fragile and unstable locations – the margins of the tectonic plates. Of considerable concern is a possible tectonic impact on the continent of Antarctica which is surrounded by plate boundaries. In fact, according to tablet evidence, Nibiru's return previously caused the ice sheet covering the Antarctic continent to destabilize and slide into the southern oceans – creating an enormous tsunami. This historic event is known as the Great Flood, or more commonly, Noah's Flood. The landmasses that were impacted in that catastrophic event comprise all those areas from the east coast of Africa to the western Indian Ocean, perhaps even extending as far east as Oceana and Australia. This is another *possible* impact of Nibiru's return.

Scientific evidence currently reports considerable destabilization of the Antarctic ice sheet from ice sheet melting already underway, bringing the historic evidence into contemporary concern.[120]   Documented melting processes support the fact that destabilizing processes are underway, not just from the margins of the ice sheet that is causing the huge ice shelves to break away, but at the continental boundary with the surface ice sheet. As surface ice melts, the released water trickles down through cracks in the ice creating flows at the bottom of the sheet. These flows weaken the entire ice sheet's attachment to the continental landmass by reducing friction.

Additionally, satellite evidence indicates that the behavior of the West Antarctic ice sheet *already* shows considerable glacier melt, prompting considerable concern on the part of scientists.[121]   While the collapse of the Larson A and B shelves[122] did not appreciably raise sea levels, accelerating glacial flows and the potential destabilization of the West Antarctic ice sheet are predicted to raise sea levels by more than 15 feet. This flooding impact would threaten hundreds of millions who live in coastal regions around the globe, and the return of Nibiru, assuming similar consequences to that caused by Noah's Flood, would increase this catastrophic impact by more than a hundred-fold. Nibiru's return could again destabilize the entire ice sheet and create globally extensive tsunamis with landmass flooding holding a significantly greater consequence than was reported in biblical historical accounts. This is more than a possible impact – it extends into the realm of *a probable one*.

Probable Planetary Impacts

Another cause of Arctic and Antarctic ice sheet melting also is providing evidence of the potential threat of Nibiru's planetary effects. Current reports of increased volcanism and earthquakes around the globe suggest increasing activity within the Earth's mantle. Coupled with the plethora of reports of global warming from rising atmospheric levels of carbon dioxide, and warming of the oceans (because of the diminution of surface ice that reflects ultra-violet radiation, thereby increasing solar warming of the ocean waters), there is a reasonable probability that the continental landmass also is warming.[123] This information supports the *probability* of a future catastrophic event – one we can say with considerable assurance *will happen again.*[124]

Likewise, increased tectonic activity caused by Nibiru's return would have its greatest deleterious effects at all the tectonic plate margins. Activity from the gravitational impacts of a large planet such as Nibiru traversing the solar system would have considerable impacts for the human inhabitants that live in proximity to these plate boundaries. Regularly, the inhabitants of these locations suffer periodic earthquakes.[125] Moreover, widespread tectonic activity coupled with increased convectional flows within Earth's mantle could produce eruptions at any – or all – of the six known super volcanoes located around the world (located at: Yellowstone, Long Valley and Valles Caldera in the U.S.; Lake Toba in North Sumatra, Indonesia; Taupo Volcano, North Island, New Zealand; and Aira Caldera, Kagoshima Prefecture, Kyushu, Japan).

A recent network science program has simulated the likely consequences to huge areas of the landmasses in the areas in proximity to these super volcanoes. These consequences would include lava flows and extensive spreading of volcanic ash. Such consequences would cause long-lasting impacts on weather that even could result in the return of an ice age.[126] Paul D. Lowman, Jr., a scientist with the NASA Goddard Space Flight Center, offers apropos advice on the probabilities outlined here and this advice suggests how we might seriously consider these probable future impacts. He recounts the well-known geologic maxim: "the present is the key to the past." The complementary adage we could consider to become a future scenario: **"The present is the key to the future."**(emphasis added here)[127]

Preferable Planetary Impacts

Preferable outcome considers personal and societal values we are willing to accept. Few – if any – of the planetary impacts discussed above can be dealt with on a societal – or even a personal – scale. In other words, we would prefer not to experience any of the outcomes outlined here. Under some of the possible and probable outcomes identified, the only choices left to Earth's inhabitants would involve moving to high altitude locations, or burrowing underground in inland locations away from oceans, and also away from large inland water basins. Each of these options hold serious problems – and expense. We know that some governmental facilities (political and military) have been constructed below ground (ostensibly to allow those functions to continue to operate in the case of asteroid impacts or nuclear war. But the scope of planetary impacts from world-wide tsunamis and super volcanic eruptions would have relatively short lead times. The most serious consequences of these two choices are coupled with the destruction of food production. No amount of food storage would avoid the probable impacts on the world's populations. While historical evidence suggests that some groups of humans survived the past ice ages, the current size of the world's population would preclude mass efforts to facilitate human survival under the potential planetary impacts discussed here.

Plausible Planetary Impacts

When we consider what *could* happen to Earth when Nibiru returns, we must take into account that it is the proximity of Nibiru's huge planetary body to Earth that would generate tectonic consequences. However, there are some *plausible* considerations that can be conjectured. If Earth's position on its ecliptic is shielded by the Sun's mass, some of the events considered in the scenarios proposed here might be mitigated. When Nibiru makes its "sling-shot" transit around the Sun, if Earth is on the opposite side with the Sun serving to attenuate Nibiru's gravitational effects, plausibly some of the effects might not be severe. We know that Nibiru has returned to Earth's portion of the solar system several times in the distant past, and a few times in the past 10,000 years (of recorded history). Volcanic eruptions have occurred, producing (perhaps) regional as well as global impacts.[128] Obviously humans have survived these returns. However, archaeological evidence does indicate that devastating tsunamis have occurred. Exactly which scenarios occurred that generated relatively benign plausible impacts we can not know because events that happened then have not become part of recorded history.

Impacts of the Return of the Anunnaki

A return of the Anunnaki will be inevitable as the planet Nibiru nears and then retreats from the vicinity our Sun. If the Anunnaki have been coming to Earth approximately every 3600 years since their first incursions to Earth 445,000 years ago, we cannot assume (under any scenario) they would not come again. The certainty of the return of the Anunnaki suggests scenarios that would give us *possible, probable, and plausible future* consequences important to consider.

We only need to be reminded that the reason the Anunnaki had for coming to Earth initially was to obtain gold. While gold still is found on Earth, though perhaps not as plentifully as it was in the previous times when they came to Earth, there is a reasonable *possibility* that they again will want gold. One thing is certain: *if* the Anunnaki want gold, and come with the intention of obtaining it, *they will take it,* regardless of the fact that currently gold deposits are under the control of several national governments who hold territorial ownership of those deposits.

Historical evidence provides several clues as to benevolent Anunnaki behavior, so we will not conjecture hostile consequences for their return.[129]   In fact, in previous visits, they made contributions to Earth's inhabitants. In a Sitchin interview he stated:

> That Mankind's progression from Paleolithic (Old Stone Age) to Mesolithic (Middle Stone Age) to Neolithic (New Stone Age) and the great Sumerian civilization had occurred in intervals of about 3600 years **is a fact**. That Anu visited Earth, approved the grant of civilization (knowledge, science, technology) to Mankind **is certain**…. (emphasis provided here).[130]

In addition to these past positive and productive contributions to human civilization, we could possibly expect additional contributions and assistance. Heaven knows we need assistance to achieve peace among Earth's peoples and nations, assistance in finding effective ways to control the growth of the population, and ways to deal with the deleterious consequences of climate change.

Sitchin with statue of an ancient immense god.
photo by Wally Motlock

Possible Outcomes

Contrary to some movie depictions of "aliens" as entities that are unfriendly, forceful, aggressive, antagonistic, and openly hostile toward humans,[131] evidence exists to show that a specific Anunnaki, namely Enki, behaved in benevolent ways toward his human creations in the past. The notable example is the evidence of preparatory instructions for building a vessel for Noah and his family to use to survive the inundation, thereby saving his small entourage from *total* extinction. This action suggests that Enki behaved benevolently toward humankind, thus it is *possible* this attitude of benevolence still exists, and that a return would bring a positive, peaceful, and as productive a visit as were several of those that occurred when the Anunnaki came previously. However, it must be pointed out that while the flood was positive for Noah and his entourage, it did cause the demise of all other humans living in various parts of the planet at that time.

Sitchin tells us that the tablets recount the reason that the humans living in Sumer were drowned. The tablet story tells of out-of-control procreation that brought the flood's dire consequences to earthlings, and it was Enki's brother Enlil's decision to wipe out all of the burgeoning population. Enlil's rage was provoked by his increasing intolerance of the disruptive noise made by the hordes who caroused near his ziggurat. So deep was Enlil's anger that he vowed to eliminate all of the earthlings. Except for Enki's creative way of giving a warning to the righteous Noah,[132] and bypassing the agreement made by Anu and the Anunnaki council to keep the impending flood a secret, *all* earthlings would have perished.[133]

There are other reasons – perhaps more pressing reasons – the Anunnaki might return to Earth. Modern technologic advancements have brought Earth's civilizations into the Nuclear Age. It is well-known that thousands of UFO sightings have focused on nuclear installations around the world.[134] A plethora of sighting evidence has been collected by the Mutual UFO Network (MUFON) at nuclear facilities.[135] Whether the observed sightings are vehicles manned by

Anunnaki, or the more frequently observed small grey robotic-like entities from any of the twelve or fourteen other suspected space-based planetary systems, evidence indicates that there definitely are some species of extraterrestrials (ETs) – perhaps Anunnaki – paying close attention to the modern population's "hell-bent" ambitions to acquire and control nuclear technology.

Probable Outcomes

The *probability* exists that the Anunnaki indeed are interested in our growing uses of nuclear technology. This is a valid assumption because of the previous use by the Anunnaki of a nuclear device on the Sinai Peninsula that provided them with knowledge of what the human consequences were in the past. This nuclear event ostensibly destroyed the "sinful" cities of Sodom and Gomorrah. Sitchin discusses this event briefly in his *12th Planet* book, and in more detail in *The End of Days* volume. In the later publication, a satellite photograph is shown of the blackened scar that still remains at that location. Sitchin indicates that the photo shows the "…immense cavity and the crack in the surface where the nuclear explosion had taken place."[136] On one of his expeditions, Sitchin guided a group of "fans" to this Sinai location, where those attending that trip observed with their own eyes the blackened rock remains on the surface of the scar. One of those "fans" indicates that the surface had an indentation of about a foot. The surrounding landscape consisted of white rock, probably limestone. An Egyptian man on this trip warned the group not to go into this scar as it had been mined during the war between Egypt and Israel.

Most importantly, several rock samples were retrieved and examined scientifically.[137] The scientific report of the analysis of those rock samples indicates that the samples document an ancient nuclear explosion. The sample rocks collected at the Sinai site contained only the isotope U-235 – and *none* of the far more prevalent isotope Uranium-238. The first conclusion the scientists drew was that the purity of the U-235 could only have resulted from purification achieved at a level our technology has not yet achieved. The second observation dealt with the plastic flow of the rocks (which basically were limestone derived from years of under sea deposition on the sea floor, but at a minimal depth of less than 1/16th inch). The surface of these rocks was impacted by a very high heat that discolored them, and caused the top layer to crack away from the limestone inner layers when the heat was applied. These rocks unquestionably were impacted with a near proximity nuclear heat source for a short duration. One researcher was forced to use a diamond saw when he attempted to cut into the (normally soft) limestone. Even though this surface layer was very thin, it was not drillable, as it had become a fused ceramic that was too hard to be penetrated. There is no support to substantiate that these sample rocks were remnants of an asteroid impact because no shock grains were found. They also are not the remnants of volcanic eruption because they are sedimentary (not igneous) rock. This report from the scientific examination is irrefutable evidence of an ancient nuclear detonation using a technology that rivals and appears to *exceed modern capability* to isotropically separate uranium species. Some of the most sensitive and state-of-the-art equipment currently available was needed to analyze these rock samples to obtain this information.

It is feasible to assume that the Anunnaki might want to avoid another catastrophe – like the Sinai event – and are taking a *benevolent* posture relative to any events involving nuclear technology accidents.[138] This bold assumption also is based on a fortuitous set of observations made following the accidental explosion in 1987 at the Chernobyl nuclear power site. These observations are reported by Dr. Vladimir Rubtsov, a Russian scientist. He reports the following information in a conference presentation.[139] He interviewed scientists who provided an incredible explanation for sightings they made of objects hovering over the Chernobyl site *before and after* the explosion. Rubtsov's report states:

> ...about one month before the Chernobyl disaster, I had a talk with an air traffic controller of the Kharkov airport. He told me that according to pilots' reports, there were a rising number of UFO observations in the area of the Chernobyl Nuclear Power Station (ChNPS). Later it became known that on the night of the fire in the ChNPS, some 3 hours after the explosion, a team of nuclear specialists saw in the sky over

the station a fiery ball of the color of brass. The witnesses estimated its diameter as 6 - 8 meters and its distance from the burning nuclear reactor No. 4 was some 300 meters. Just before the observation these specialists measured the level of radiation in the place where they were standing. It was measured at 3000 miliroentgens per hour. Suddenly two bright rays of crimson color extended from the ball to the reactor.... This lasted for some 3 minutes. The rays abruptly faded and the ball slowly floated away in a north-westerly direction.... Then we again looked at our radiation monitor. It displayed *only* 800 miliroentgens per hour.

How can we explain this report? It would appear, to this writer and to those Russian scientists as well, that an extremely rare event occurred. A *deliberate* **reduction** in the amount of radiation measured at the site took place, and it was "a fiery ball of the color of brass" that did it. The only phenomenon that could account for such an action is a UFO. The action of this hovering vehicle is what we call a *plausible* explanation. We might infer that intelligent observers (from space) were monitoring this site *before the fire and explosion* and took palliative action after the event. Knowing the enormous human repercussions of the extremely high initial level of radioactivity, and in a *benevolent action,* they enacted an extraction process to mitigate (reduce) the level of radiation. As enigmatic as this report is, with Sitchin's explanation of the ancient benevolence of Enki toward his "creations," it is possible another act of benevolence has occurred.

Additionally, we must admit that the U.S. military has treated whoever it is that is visiting Earth with aggressive hostile actions.[140] New evidence has come forward to indicate that the UFO crash at Roswell in 1947 was *caused by* the U.S. military. That space vehicle was shot down by a then newly developed military beam that disrupted the electromagnetic propulsion capability of the UFO.[141] We need to consider the possibility that military responses will either precede political ones, or be employed by political decision-makers. Unlike in the movies, the consequences would not be positive.

Preferable Outcomes

Because preferable outcomes deal with *what should be*, we must look critically at the aggressive actions taken by the U.S. military who initially responded to UFO sightings. The initial reactions likely were based on the assumption that these previously unrecognized vehicles were "invading" our airspace, and that they likely held hostile intent. Aggression and attempts to intercept UFOs were logical reactions, considering, in the case of the Roswell event, in 1947, we had just come through a war. However, when the military discovered that our weapons were useless against the superior speed and maneuverability of the UFOs, they seemingly abandoned their attack posture.[142]

It certainly would be *preferable* to take a benevolent non-hostile posture toward UFOs, especially in light of all the ancient evidence – and also some modern evidence – that indicates that the ET UFO technology is far superior to ours. We (as far as the public is concerned) have not yet developed viable ways to mitigate the influence of gravity.[143] However, aliens seem to have done this. We still expend enormous energy and financial resources to put our vehicles and payloads into space. The ETs also have the knowledge – and technological know how – that allows them to "slip" between dimensions, and to traverse enormous interstellar distances. It *would be preferable* to wait for the Anunnaki to return and let them teach us how to successfully accomplish these challenges. We don't know if the UFOs are piloted by Anunnaki, but if they are, they were generous with their advice on how to get civilizations going in the past, perhaps they will assist us again. We probably should assume they again would be generous in the future if we "cease and desist" from taking aggressive military action when they arrive.

There are those among us who are conceptually incapable of working with future-oriented scenarios, or more likely, who want human energy and resources to be focused *only* on earthly problems such as poverty, military security, abatement of war, control of disease and pestilence, to mitigate and control pollution, and manage successfully the ecology of Earth, especially under continuing population growth. The most stimulating scenarios, *the preferable ones*, are attractive because they are positive, and because they are not based on fear, an emotion that immobilizes thoughts and slows and disrupts one's creative energies. We need a positive perspective to develop enlightening possible and plausible outcomes that would move humankind forward, thereby allowing us to become a more intelligent, humane, and spiritually developed species. Those scenarios that meet these progressive future-oriented positive goals are the preferable ones – the ones most difficult to identify and extrapolate into our near or even distant future.

Those that hold onto "gloom and doom" possible outcomes do little to encourage positive mental energy that is useful and indeed necessary for a creative, productive, healthful, and safe future. The Earth-centric viewpoint ignores the reality that *we are **not** alone in the Universe*. A line taken from the movie *Contact* is most appropriate here: ***If we are alone in the Universe, it's an awful waste of space.***[144]

Nothing in life is to be feared, it is only to be understood.
Now is the time to understand more,
so that we may fear less.

—Quote from Marie Curie

AFTERWORD

New knowledge should ennoble not merely
those who seek and find it;
... it should add to the civility and wonder
and the nobility of the common life.

—J. Robert Oppenheimer, in
The Need for New Knowledge

If you know in your heart what you are looking for,
*and believe it – it **is** true.*

—Dialogue by character Mike Reagan,
played by James Craig, in
the movie *Lost Angel.*

What is especially notable about the impact and implications of Sitchin's works, research findings, conference and seminar presentations, and personal contributions, is the scope of topics he explored and discussed. He was an indefatigable researcher. In his series of weekend seminars, conducted in the beginning decade of the 21st century, he knew that many of his "fans" were attending one event after the other, so he prepared new material to make each lecture a noteworthy learning experience. What is particularly important is the impact of the man himself on every individual who knew him. Especially to his devoted "fans," he was a personal friend and revered teacher.

It is heartwarming that in 2010 Zecharia Sitchin received two notable awards in recognition of his lifetime of study, research, and numerous publications. In February 2010, his accomplishments were celebrated at a special luncheon at the Conscious Life Expo held in Los Angeles.

Radio host George Noory of the "Coast to Coast" radio program presented Zecharia with a lifetime achievement award. Additionally, a personal letter of acclaim was read from Erich von Daniken, author of *Chariots of the Gods* and other ancient astronaut publications.

Then in May, 2010, Zecharia received a particularly notable achievement award from the founders of the Middle East Research Center LTD, presented to him at a luncheon ceremony held in Washington, DC. A highlight of this event, following the presentation of the award, was Sitchin's two-hour lecture to an audience of over 150 attendees, in which he presented highlights from his accumulated research findings.

The stated objective of this book is to illuminate, highlight, and celebrate the extraordinary contribution of Zecharia Sitchin. It is sadly noteworthy that Zecharia Sitchin passed away on October 9, 2010, just three months after his 90th birthday. His creative energies were obvious up to that event. He leaves a life-long effort to unravel, interpret, explain, and promulgate the authentic meanings embedded in the ancient Sumerian tablets as a legacy. His several books, numerous conference presentations and workshops represent his efforts to share with the world this knowledge. These efforts are deserving of the highest accolades.

But, he did more than just teach his readers and "fans" what he learned. To the devoted individuals who found his work educational, stimulating, enlightening, and personally rewarding, he also gave his friendship. It is apropos here to share some of the comments this writer received when several Sitchin friends were asked to articulate their thoughts on the contribution he had on their thinking, and on their lives.

A rare photo of Sitchin's elusive smile. He made true friends of his biggest fans.
Zecharia, you are loved and will be missed.   photo courtesy of Lena Jacobson

The following commentaries show that Sitchin's legacy cuts across all walks of life and deeply affected those who knew him. We now report the commentaries of several Sitchin friends.

A devoted "Sitchinite" whose career focuses on the media production arena, shared these thoughts:

> Zecharia Sitchin's work has helped me to recognize my life's mission. Through his work, I have become inspired to play a part in helping people realize that "we are not alone in the universe." We all must strive to reach this realization so that the whole of humanity progresses in a peaceful and intelligent way into the future. Zecharia Sitchin's work provides a doorway through which we can examine our ancient history by bringing forward what previously has been overlooked. Those of us fortunate enough to have known Zecharia in a personal way have found his advice about the skeptics, while disdainful, also motivating. He told me:

"If they don't believe you, show them a cylinder seal, or a recipe for beer, or some architectural plans from 4600 BCE Sumer." Zecharia has given us courage as well as a wonderful education. (Jenn S.)

Another Sitchin "fan" follows, whose work-life was spent in an auto factory and whose personal interests attracted him to Sitchin's work. He also traveled on several expeditions with Sitchin. He writes:

Zecharia Sitchin has made mankind aware of the actual history of our planet. He has contributed a lifetime to research that enlightens us all. In the time I have known him, he has broadened my knowledge and made my life much richer and more fulfilling. He truly is a pioneer and a trailblazer. In the words of the Star Trek program's introduction – he has *gone where no man has gone before.* I will never forget him. (Zbig B.)

The fellow who served as Zecharia Sitchin's official photographer on nearly all of his journeys and expeditions, and whose career focused on the business he owned, wrote the following:

Zecharia Sitchin was my guru and my hero! More than any other teacher or professor, he has helped me make sense out of the chaos in the information about history, religion, etymology, ancient engineering, and technology. His writings made total sense to me and have given me many "aha " moments. As in all his books and on our "fact finding" trips, his attention to detail greatly impressed me, and provided the physical proof I needed to fully understand. He also provided the proof that I needed to make that information my own. There is no doubt in my mind that knowing Zecharia Sitchin has enriched my life. When I "grow up" in wisdom, I want to be like Zecharia. His endeavor focused on the Goddess of Ur Genome Project is the crowning jewel of his life, and I want this project to be successful. (Wally M.)

The next quote comes from an extremely bright, energetic, cerebral engineer-type fellow who first encountered Sitchin's ideas in a book he discovered on a bookstore shelf nearly 20 years ago, and who became so interested in the man that he found ways to interrupt his demanding work to travel with Zecharia. He recounts his reactions and explains the tremendous impact of Zecharia Sitchin's writings on his curiosity. He shares these thoughts:

> I expected the first book I found, *When Time Began*, to be just another discussion that presented something like "we couldn't do this at that time, so it had to be aliens." But Zecharia Sitchin's books were peppered with external resources and translations of tablets that had been found only in the past two hundred years. He related the significance of these artifacts. For me, his writings started a huge intellectual awakening. First I had to explore ancient history, then linguistics, followed by phonetics, philology, then self-training in cuneiform and Akkadian grammar. Those topics led to specialty research on metallurgy, location of ores, and how the refining and development of alloys was done. Each of those topics led to questioning how ancient people first began figuring out what was dirt and what was ore, how to safely dig mines deep into the ground, how to get into and out of those mines with that ore, how to refine the ore and make metals, and how to process it. For each topic I encountered in Sitchin's books, I was prompted to break it down into finite learning steps, only to discover that each step required a huge amount of associated knowledge to have progressed to that step.
>
> The result was an amazing learning journey that Zecharia initiated for me through his books. I learned enough to be able to discuss a large array of topics and to make my own educated observations and deductions. That process still, 20 years later, is ongoing and has made my life much more interesting. To cover many of Sitchin's topics, as presented in his writings, I have traveled down an enlightening personal growth path, so I can't thank Zecharia enough. His work has made my life infinitely richer and more stimulating. (Barry B.)

Another notable testimonial came from a woman, who after hearing of Zecharia Sitchin's passing, shared his impact on her life, a response that summarizes his influence on numerous other Sitchin "fans." She worked originally as a travel agent, and her enthusiasm for travel again was sparked when she read Sitchin's books and learned of his tours. She renewed her excitement about overseas travel by participating in several of the Sitchin expeditions. She tells us:

> Reading Zecharia Sitchin's books created a huge change in my life. Thereafter, all I read and heard about in the fields of science, religion, social science and even psychiatry, was filtered through the implications laid out by Zecharia. He brought the world of ancient events to my reality. To know Zecharia Sitchin was to marvel at and greatly appreciate his great intellect. I admired his tenacity, his single-mindedness in study, and his ability to translate and report such esoteric material so that anyone could read and understand it. What a loss to this world that his voice no longer will be heard. Thankfully we have his books. Those of us who knew and loved this man have a void in our lives difficult to deal with, and even more difficult to explain. His books will continue to provide illumination to the world, I'm sure. To my dear friend and teacher, I wish the immortality that Gilgamesh sought. (Joyce T.)

Still another devoted Sitchinite shares her thoughts:

> Zecharia Sitchin was – no, is, because he continues to live in our hearts – a man of such brilliance, perseverance, strength, insight, understanding, wit and kindness, was also humble, but he called himself *only* a reporter. I am saddened that he did not receive the recognition he so justly deserved in his lifetime, particularly from the scientific community, but his "fans" (as he calls us) will see to it that recognition is bestowed on him. With the success of the Goddess of Ur Genome Project, that long-deserved recognition will be

given to him. The world then will know that he wrote only
the truth. I will forever hold him in my heart and be grateful
I was allowed to call him my teacher and my friend. (Suzie
S.)

And finally, a loyal Sitchin "fan" who has carried out her illustrious
career as an engineer shares these perspectives:

Zecharia Sitchin changed my frame of reference, of both
time and space. He elucidated a most crucial issue that has
occupied my thoughts: what is the origin of planet Earth and
its people? This makes Sitchin a person of prophetic stature,
a reincarnation of the prophet Zecharia. The time came and
the prophet was called to say what really happened. Sitchin
revealed what the stone stele and Sumerian clay tablets were
silently telling us for several thousand years. He made them
speak in a poignant voice. Sitchin reported their story about
the cradle of our civilization with such an authentic voice
that we experience all the thousands of years since Sumer
in our own time. In addition, like no other in the history
of this planet, he positioned our planet in the Universe and
showed its connection to other planets – and beyond. He let
us know that we are not alone and thus he changed our time-
space frame of reference. We learned from him the cosmic
history of Earth, and thanks to his works, we now know what
the Anunnaki told the Sumerians. We now know also to
which "god" we owe our strengths and weaknesses. Most
importantly, Zecharia Sitchin convincingly demythologized
history. He changed both our view of the past and our
perspectives for the future. For all these things I will be
forever grateful to Zecharia, who shared knowledge about
the connection of Heaven with Earth. This makes him not
only a prophet, but *the greatest historian of our time.* (Lena
J-M.)

These voices from just a small sample of individuals who personally
knew Zecharia Sitchin characterize the feelings of hundreds of others.

It is a rare event in one's life to have the opportunity to witness genius in action. Knowing Zecharia Sitchin, has given us this great honor.

The Sitchin paradigm has made an enormous contribution to the intellectual lives of a small portion of people who were energized by his expertise, energy, and spirit. This contribution continues within the future actions of his friends and fans. We now need to demonstrate our appreciation for his contribution by furthering his work in whatever ways are available to us. We can do this by celebrating his work, and continuing to do so in the years to come.

Much has been written and said about Zecharia Sitchin, but there is still more to say – lest the world forgets. In the words of a well known space explorer who made exploration of space a household idea –

Make it so! [145]

APPENDIX A

The Legacy of Zecharia Sitchin[1]

by Jack Barranger

In 1976 Zecharia Sitchin published a book which would be one of the seeds spawning revolution in the way humans would look at their own past. This book, *The 12ᵗʰ Planet*, would challenge much of our consensus reality about what is myth and what is actual history.

With numerous books published, Sitchin has, in the years since *The 12ᵗʰ Planet* (1976), moved from obscure scholar to a lecturer who is in great demand. He is a mild-mannered man whose style is more academic than flamboyant. Yet what he writes about is capable of shattering the foundations of our collective belief systems. Sitchin operates from a highly revolutionary thesis: what you thought was mythology is actually history. In many cases, all those gods mentioned in myth after myth were real, and they made a considerable impact on the emerging human race.

My own introduction to Sitchin came when I thought I had picked up a "safe" historical book titled *The Stairway to Heaven* that Sitchin published in 1980. I thought that I was going to read more deeply into one of my favorite mythological writings: *The Epic of Gilgamesh*. However, 60 pages into this work I read the following:

---

1 Originally published by The Book Tree in 1996 and is currently out of print.

> Because the Anunnaki (the so called gods of mythology) were close to revolt, they made a decision to create a race of beings which would do the difficult work in the mines. This slave race turned out to be the human race.

That rocked me. Not because it was absurd, but instead because it explained what I had been experiencing with many of the 400 interviews I had been conducting for my previous book, *Knowing When to Quit*. I had sensed an inability by these people to pursue and embrace what they *really* wanted to do with their lives. I found many who appeared to be stuck in a slave mentality. Their work was more of an obligation than fulfillment. They expected to serve and – despite misery in their work – found it very hard to break free and search for something better.

Could Zecharia Sitchin be onto something? Could his research possibly explain what I saw as a "slave chip" mentality? Is it possible that many people continue to lead highly limited lives because thousands of years ago they were programmed to be slaves?

I began reading his other books like *The 12th Planet* and *The Wars of Gods and Men* to see if he could offer further insights. I was not disappointed. In his highly researched books with impeccable academic documentation, Sitchin had advanced the thesis that what we previously considered to be mythology may actually be history.

Slightly more than one hundred years ago, Hermann Schliemann stunned the academic world by providing evidence that the Trojan War actually happened. In the 1960s an American group of explorers used Homer's *Odyssey* as a guidebook and found that they were able to follow the oceanic currents as described in that work and land where Odysseus landed. These and other ventures began putting a crack in the consensus reality that mythology was simply "myth."

As an authority on ancient history, and one of only 200 scholars who could read and interpret the Sumerian language (in addition to

Hebrew), Zecharia Sitchin is uniquely qualified to address this kind of issue. As both a scholar and an archaeologist, he is highly respected in academic circles. His revolutionary first book, *The 12ᵗʰ Planet*, came out in 1976 and was read mainly by scholars and lay people willing to embrace the thesis that the Hebrew, Greek, Sumerian, and Babylonian myths were not simply inventions of emerging cultures – but were instead historical accounts.

> There were no more local deities. They were gods – active and present on Earth even before there were men upon Earth. Indeed, the very existence of Man was deemed to have been the result of a deliberate creative enterprise on the part of the gods.
>
> —Sitchin, *The 12ᵗʰ Planet*

This idea is not exactly new. Some archaeologists began exploring this theory in the late 19ᵗʰ century. However, it was not until the late 1960s and into the 1970s that Erich von Daniken with his *Chariots of the Gods* and other spin-off books successfully brought the ancient astronaut theory into the mainstream. The idea mainly stated that astronauts from another planet or star system visited Earth and significantly impacted the advancement of the human race. However, von Daniken hurt his credibility by seeing examples of spaceships and astronauts in space gear in far too many ancient carvings and pictures. This – and the lack of readiness of Americans to consider this possibility – caused von Daniken to fall from grace.

After the publication of Sitchin's *The 12ᵗʰ Planet*, more than ten years passed before its ideas began spawning a revolution in human thought. This was a far more scholarly work than von Daniken's. One basis for Sitchin's work was that a large inhabited planet in our solar system circled the sun in an extreme ellipsis. He did not make this up – it is recorded in ancient texts like the *Enuma Elish: The Seven Tablets of Creation* (translated by L.W. King) the *Atrahasis* (a book which most scholars and theologians admit was the foundation for the first six chapters of Genesis) and the Sumerian *Karsag Epics* [a series of tablets from Nippur collected and translated by Christian O'Brien].

The ancient Sumerians called this planet Niburu. According to these epics, every 3600 years this planet would enter the circumference of our solar system. As the planet approached, highly advanced beings would leave Niburu and come to Earth. They, in fact, colonized it.

For those who struggle with this as I did, less than 20 years ago astronomers at UCLA determined that a large planet is circling the sun in extreme ellipsis. They were able to determine this by the gravitational anomalies recorded in the circling of the other eight planets. Could this be the Niburu of the supposedly mythological texts? If the reality of this planet turns out to be true, then could the fact that this planet was inhabited also be a reality? If this newly discovered planet is indeed inhabited, could its inhabitants be the creators of the human race?

That is the question which many scientists are willing to consider. Once a week, 150 top scientists meet on-line (conferencing by computer) to share their latest insights and discoveries which support what they refer to as the *Nefilim Thesis* – the idea that advanced beings created humanity.

The word *Nefilim* is used in Genesis 6:4.

> There were giants in the earth in those days; and also after that, when the sons of God came unto the daughters of men, and they bare children to them....   —King James Bible

Sitchin makes it clear in all his books that "giants" is a mistranslation and that the word Nefilim actually means "those who came down from the sky." That is how the word is translated in the *Atrahasis* (which the Hebrews drew on for the first six chapters of Genesis).

Some other questions from our ancient past continue to haunt us. The largest of these is related to evolution. Despite Darwin and all who have followed, no one has been able to explain how Neanderthal man advanced so quickly to Cro-Magnon man. Considering how slowly Neanderthal man was advancing, the very quick evolutionary leap to Cro-Magnon man was highly unlikely. Science now shows convincing evidence of both Cro-Magnon and Neanderthals living, for a while, during the same period! This makes sense. Should the "experiment" go wrong, an advanced race would not want to eradicate the original race too quickly. Even so, Homo Neanderthalis was totally destroyed within two thousand years after the introduction of Cro-Magnon man – something considered "naturally impossible" based on the long, slow process of evolution. What really happened here?

Zecharia Sitchin does not believe that Cro-Magnon man was solely a product of evolution, but of genetic engineering. His indefatigable research has led him to this conclusion:

> Here then is the answer to the puzzle: the Nefilim did not "create" man out of nothing; rather they took an existing creature and manipulated it, to "bind upon it" the "image of the god."
>
> —Sitchin, *The 12ᵗʰ Planet*

"What!" exclaim the skeptical. "Not even von Daniken went that far!" Actually, von Daniken did go that far, but America was no longer listening. Despite increased research skills and more credible support, the last seven books of von Daniken have not been able to find a publisher in America (unlike in a more open-minded Europe).

Sitchin's first book, *The 12ᵗʰ Planet*, has what von Daniken's first few books lacked: impeccable scholarship. From his translation of the *Atrahasis* and recently discovered tablets of *The Epic of Gilgamesh*, Sitchin relates how the Anunnaki were mining on planet Earth and the leaders realized they were on the brink of mutiny. As written by humans, the stories told of the Anunnaki's increasing problem:

> When the gods, like men, bore the work and suffered the toil,
> the toil of the gods was great, the work was heavy and the
> distress was much.   —*Atrahasis*

The *Atrahasis* relates in vivid detail how the main leaders of the Anunnaki debated and determined how they would solve this problem. They were far from home and realized that harsh disciplinary measures would be counterproductive. Finally, they agreed on a solution:

> Let a Lulu (primitive worker) be created.
> Let him bear the yoke
> Let him carry the toil of the gods.

From this ancient work, used by the Hebrews for Genesis, comes a tale of how the ancient gods saw a potential problem and then solved it by creating a new species – a feat of genetic engineering. If the Hebrews did indeed take material from the *Atrahasis* and place it into the first chapters of Genesis, why did they fail to include something this important?

How interesting that people will say something is true if it comes from the Bible, yet will balk at the idea of advanced beings inhabiting the planet found in other credible texts, but not mentioned in the Bible. For example, we teach our children that Jehovah was real, but the Greek god Zeus was not. For centuries we believed that Moses parted the Red Sea based on just a few Biblical verses. Until recently we believed that the now proven ten year Trojan War was simply myth. Into the fray of this dichotomy comes Zecharia Sitchin who claims that not only were Zeus and Jehovah real, but they were most likely the same entity. In fact, he takes this idea one step further by claiming that Enlil, one of the main characters of the Sumerian *Atrahasis*, was the foundation for both Zeus and Jehovah.

The subtitle of the *Atrahasis* is *The Babylonian Story of the Flood*. Sitchin found some interesting parallels in this version of the flood and the Biblical account. In the *Atrahasis,* Enlil declares that he has had enough of this newly created human race – they complain, they rebel, and they make so much noise that he could not sleep at night.

> The god Enlil said to the other gods:
> "oppressive have become the
> Pronouncements of mankind
> Their conjugations deprive me of sleep."

His solution: get rid of them. His method: take advantage of an oncoming natural disaster. He knew the great flood was coming.

However, Enlil's brother, Enki , was *relatively* more compassionate. He went to the human, Utnapishtim (Noah), and told him to build a boat which would survive a large flood. Enki told this human that he (Utnapishtim) will know the flood is coming when he saw their "sky vehicles" departing. For some reason, the Hebrews decided not to put that small part in Genesis.

The *Atrahasis* has far greater detail and description of the flood. It tells of Enki, Enlil, and the other Anunnaki gods hovering high above in their vehicles, watching the encroaching flood destroy their human creations. Many of them weep and wonder if they have done the right thing. They watch in horror as millions drown. The *Atrahasis* goes on to tell how Enki reveals to the Anunnaki that he has saved Utnapishtim and some of his followers. Enlil is at first enraged, but later is consoled by the fact that some of their creations actually will survive.

Is Zecharia Sitchin starting a revolution? Yes, because he is introducing academically solid evidence that highly advanced beings were here in the flesh over 4000 years ago. He is compounding that revolution by offering solid written evidence – some of it discovered in the last 25 years – that we as humans were created as a workforce to fulfill the will of the gods. Backed by evidence from *The Epic of Gilgamesh*, the *Karsag Epics*, and the *Atrahasis*, we are able to see with a much greater depth what happened during the time that these advanced beings were here.

Much of this is not pretty. Relegating this to the realm of myth would ease the pain. However, Sitchin claims that we must boldly look at our past if we are going to advance as humans. We were programmed to be slaves. Sitchin and his contemporaries suggest that this programming remains with us today (Neil Freer covers this aspect very effectively in his book *Breaking the Godspell*).

One area where Sitchin's scholarship takes a Biblical area to a new level is in the story of the Tower of Babel. The Biblical account, according to the Hebrews, gives the impression that a group of humans were building this tower so they could get closer to the heavens. Sitchin, after many years of probing into the Hebrew and Sumerian languages, feels that the Genesis account does not give the full story. A clearer understanding of the Tower of Babel incident might lie in the more descriptive *Atrahasis*. According to this source, the humans were not building a tower. They were actually building a rocket ship. Because the Anunnaki feared these newly created beings might actually get off the planet and travel to Niburu, the Anunnaki took drastic measures:

> Come, let us go down and confound their language,
> that they might not understand one another's speech.
> —Genesis 11:7

Yes, this last example is from the Bible, and this is the main source for Sitchin's claim. He centers his revolutionary thesis around the Hebrew word "shem," which most Bible scholars believe to be the word for tower. However, Sitchin – because of his Sumerian studies and references made to this event in the *Atrahasis – believes that the word "shem" actually means "rocket launching place."*

The *Atrahasis* suggests that the first human creations were frighteningly intelligent. They balked at the idea of menial work. They questioned that the Anunnaki were gods. Deceiving these newly created humans was very difficult. The thrust of the Bible suggests that man was like this because he was flawed and wicked. However, the *Atrahasis* suggests that man was like this because he was highly perceptive and immensely intelligent.

As strange as this might appear, this is not a new idea – nor is it an idea linked strictly to the history of the Mid-East. An eerie parallel is found in the Maya sacred book, the *Popul Vuh*. After creating a new species, these gods also became concerned:

> We have already tried with our first creations, our first creatures, but we could not make them praise and venerate us. So let us try to make obedient, respectful beings who will nourish and sustain us. —The *Popul Vuh*

Halfway around the world, another group of gods were becoming distressed with what they had created. Can we simply write this off as mythology? Could it be that we humans were far more intelligent than expected? Is it possible we were far too intelligent for our own good?

> ...they saw and instantly they could see far, they succeeded in seeing, they succeeded in knowing all there is in the world. When they looked, they instantly saw all around them, and they contemplated in turn the arch of heaven and the round face of the earth.   —The *Popul Vuh*

Could these newly created humans have been so intelligent that they could know more than they were expected to know? Could these newly created beings have been so intelligent that they could build a space ship which would lift them free of their toil?

The *Popul Vuh* tells of six different creations being necessary before they created a human which would serve and venerate them. It finally claims, "Their eyes were covered and they could see only that which was close...." The Bible, in a parallel sense, claims that humans had their language confounded and that they were "... scattered abroad upon the face of the Earth."

Of course, it is very simple to claim that Sitchin is a misguided scholar and relegate him to the same niche as Erich von Daniken. However, as von Daniken had some good evidence to support his theories, Sitchin has added fuel and is fanning the flames. Archaeological evidence has been and is being discovered which lends credence to the thesis that ancient astronauts were indeed here approximately four to six thousand years ago.

One of the ancient Sumerian gods, mural in a Turkish museum. The horned headress symbolized deity, note also the wings and curious wrist band.

photo courtesy of Gaye and Sergio Lub

Sitchin quietly adds evidence to this thesis with each new book. They show an indefatigable scholarship centered strongly in his own personal integrity. Like the diminishing breed of journalists who will not use material until it is solidly confirmed, Sitchin will put nothing in any of his books until he has researched the material thoroughly and verified his findings with support from several sources. Considering the revolutionary nature of Sitchin's writings, one wonders what he has discovered but cannot reveal until he completes his search for more confirmation.

One gets a hint of this in his 1990 book, *Genesis Revisited*. There, the academic scholar leapt into a new realm and claimed that not only had humanity's creators been the Anunnaki of the past, but that those same Anunnaki were on their way back. The safe, staid Sitchin now was claiming that these "creators" would return and expect us to be their slaves once again.

A 1953 government report claims that 90 percent of humanity would worship these beings. Having interviewed over 40 abductees for articles about alien abductions, I confess to wondering if a link doesn't exist between current UFO activity and the possibility of a return of the gods.

Sitchin has not disappointed me in stating that

> UFO sightings and/or abduction reports describe the occupants of those vehicles as humanoid, but not exactly human .... Exactly such beings were depicted in antiquity... humanoids sent ahead to perform special tasks.
>
> —Sitchin, *International UFO Library*, April/May 1994

In Sitchin's recent works, he speaks a bit more directly on the imminent return of the Anunnaki. He breaks free of focusing mainly on the past and suggests that we can possibly expect this in our future. Focusing on the latest Mars discoveries and the failed mission of the Mars observer, Sitchin addresses the present:

> As I brought out *Genesis Revisited* in 1990, Soviet mission controllers interpreted the spacecraft's signals as indicating that the vehicle suddenly went into a spin as if it was hit by something.... I suggest that the loss of Phobos 2 was not an accident but an incident – the deliberate shooting down of a spacecraft from Earth by someone on Mars who does not wish to be disturbed....
>
> —Sitchin, *International UFO Library*, April/May 1994

As I continue to give lectures and radio interviews on my book *Knowing When to Quit*, I sense that something has to be responsible for humanity's passion for self-limitation. As I go into my seventh year of teaching critical thinking on a college campus, I realize that dumbing down is something which comes all too easily. Perhaps a "slave chip" archetype plays over and over at the deepest levels of our consciousness. Perhaps dumbing down comes easier as we remember what happened way back in history (punishment from the gods), when we got too close.

Yet our human growth may actually come from facing our past squarely. Accepting that we were created as slaves will not be fun. However, it might be the first logical step in breaking free of a highly limiting condition which has throttled our souls for at least 4000 years. George Santayana's quote is instructive: "Those who cannot learn from the past are doomed to repeat it."

When we look at the horrors of the Holocaust and the more recent horrors of Serbian " ethnic cleansing," we might just begin to understand that these actions emanate from a much darker history. The *Atrahasis*, the *Karsag Epics*, the *Popul Vuh*, and even the *Old Testament* all speak of genocide and mass murder. The *Bhgagavad Gita* has Krishna urging Arjuna to go into battle; however, Arjuna doesn't want to fight and has to be goaded by Krishna. Other sacred books tell of mass murder and genocide as if it were something holy.

Perhaps the time is right to consider that this was never a good idea – that entities which we thought were benevolent gods tricked us into doing their labor and eventually tricked us into fighting their battles (see Sitchin's book, *The Wars of Gods and Men*).

With the scholarship of Zecharia Sitchin and other authors who are walking on the trail he has blazed, we might for the first time come to realize that what has been conditioned into us as being the truth actually cannot stand up to the light of truth.

The Russian mystic Gurdjieff claimed, "One cannot get out of prison until he is willing to admit that he is indeed in prison."

If Zecharia Sitchin is right, we were created – and conditioned – to be slaves. That is the bad news. The good news is that our slave masters departed long ago and we are, for the most part, free to search for the truth without fear.

Throughout history, many who have been conditioned to be slaves have been falsely forced to equate this slavery to holiness and spirituality. During the Inquisition, the ruling class of ersatz Anunnaki priests kept the passion for slavery-in-the-name-of-holiness alive. Today, Islamic and Christian fundamentalists alike rattle their swords in the name of "obedience equals freedom." But remember, in reference to the above Gurdjieff quote, that blind obedience is the worst form of slavery.

Many have predicted that we are fast approaching a time where a passion for freedom will erupt throughout the world. At that time, we will boldly explore our true origins, accept what is valid, and reject what is not. I believe the person who is willing to accept that Zecharia Sitchin just might be onto something is centered in the truth. This coming period could be quite exciting. Hopefully, we will be able to break free of our slave programming. Should the Anunnaki return to discover that their creations are once again out of control, we need to stand up for ourselves and cast out the cosmic manipulators, the ones who tampered with humanity and its genetic code.

The paradox of it all is that because of this tampering we now have enough godly attributes as a species to be something beyond mere slaves. Like the people in the Tower of Babel incident, and thanks largely to Sitchin, we have begun to pull away the veil that hides the truth.

Once the truth about us is fully revealed, will our society squander it, cover it up, and refuse to accept it? Maybe. If that is the case, we will never advance as a species and are destined to repeat the same failure we experienced with the Tower of Babel.

On the other hand, if we become open to the truth and have scientists and media speak out (in addition to Sitchin) on these real and shocking discoveries, then we stand a chance to prove that we have matured enough to be more than just slaves for a technologically advanced race.

To date (1996), Sitchin has sold over 12 million books and his work still continues. In conversations I have had with him at some of his workshops I attended, he has made it clear that he does not pass on any of his research until he feels that he is rock solid in his documentation and research. So what more does he know?

Zecharia Sitchin most certainly knows more, yet feels he must research further. If only we could entreat him to tell us: will we be brave enough to embrace what he has said in print and in person? If not, can we afford the price of not knowing?

The works of Zecharia Sitchin have allowed us to put many difficult puzzle pieces together regarding our fragmented and mysterious past. As long as people study his research in the future, we can expect a clearer picture to emerge as to who we really are, where we came from, and where we as a species might be going.

APPENDIX B

Memories and Highlights

At the Temple of the Seven Dolls, Dzibilchaltun, Yucatan, Mexico, 1996, explaining how, at the Spring equinox, the sun comes up through the rear window of the temple, facing his back, goes out the front and extends down the entire main walkway of the complex. Seven figurines were discovered here, all wearing strange back-packs, that can be viewed at the site's museum.   *photo by Paul Tice*

With the "Starman" statue at the Merida Museum, Mexico. Clad in a helmet and tight-fitting suit with what looks like scales, this being cradles a large five-pointed star under it's right arm. Belts draped over the top of the suit hold a strange circular device to it's belly, which some scholars have identified as belonging to water gods. Sitchin believes it to be Oannes, whose Sumerian equivalent is Ea/ Enki. Known locally as Itzamna, the name means "He Whose Home Is Water." According to legend, Itzamna and Oannes had originally waded ashore. This statue was found in northwestern Yucatan, an area said to be his final resting place.   photo by Paul Tice

In front of Toltec statue in Mexico showing possible goggles with crest of a bird motif on it's chest.

photo courtesy of Lena Jacobson

In Hattusas, meaning "City of a Thousand Gods," ancient Hittite capital during 2nd millennium BCE, in north-central Turkey. Note precise, pointed fitting of uppermost stone.

photo courtesy of Gaye and Sergio Lub

Despite being buried this is a huge, massive block, found in the walls of Troy, western Turkey.

photo courtesy of Gaye and Sergio Lub

Group that explored Turkey with Zecharia Sitchin.

photo courtesy of Gaye and Sergio Lub

With wife Rina at Trojan horse monument, Turkey.

photo courtesy of Gaye and Sergio Lub

Author with Avebury Guardian Stone, also known as Stone 10, southwestern section of the Great Circle at Avebury henge, Wiltshire, U.K.   photo courtesy of the author

Sitting in the "Devil's Chair," a carved out seat on south-facing side of Stone 1 of the Great Circle at Avebury henge, Wiltshire, U.K.

photo courtesy of the author

Sitchin and cameraman Tice (far left) prepare to enter western wall tunnel directly adjacent to the sacred Wailing Wall.   photo courtesy of Gaye and Sergio Lub

Inside the tunnel Sitchin (pointing) inspects one of three mammoth foundation stones similar to those found at Baalbek. Hidden here for centuries, each one weighs an estimated 600 tons.   photo by Paul Tice

With statue of Sumerian King Itur-Samagan of Mari, circa 2500 B.C.

photo courtesy of Gaye and Sergio Lub

On the bank of the Euphrates River

photo courtesy of Gaye and Sergio Lub

Group that explored Syria with Zecharia Sitchin.

photo courtesy of Wally Motloch

With wife Rina, in Israel

photo courtesy of Gaye and Sergio Lub

ENDNOTES

PREFACE

1   The interview cited here is reported by Antonio Huneeus in his paper "Exploring the Anunnaki-UFO Link," published in the proceedings of the First Sitchin Studies Day. That volume is titled *Of Heaven and Earth,* and was published by The Book Tree in 1996. The Huneeus chapter explores a plethora of evidence documenting UFO visits to Earth throughout history.

2   Huneeus, *Of Heaven and Earth,* p. 136.

3   The transcript of Sitchin's talk as a member of this conference's Future Panel is published by: the Human Potential Foundation, (Falls Church, VA: The *Proceedings: When Cosmic Cultures Meet,* 1995), p. 305-307.

4   Ibid. p. 305.

5   Ibid.

6   This legend's text is given in Steve Blaimer's book, *The Irish Celtic Magical Tradition.* (London: Aquarian Press, 1992).

7   While some sources indicate that the Tuatha de Danann left Ireland, other sources indicate they went underground. Likely, this is the source of the Irish belief in the "little people."

8   This trip is discussed in the Sitchin book titled *Earth Chronicles Expeditions* (Rochester Vermont: Bear & Company, 2007), pp. 28-46.

9   Miguel Angel Vergara Calleros, *Chichen-Itze: The Cosmic University of the Mayas.* (Merida, Yucatan, Mexico, 1998)

10   Zecharia Sitchin, *The End of Days: Armageddon and Prophecies of the Return* (New York: William Morrow, 2007), p 324.

11   In Sitchin's volume titled *Journeys to the Mythical Past*, he discusses his efforts to gain access to the Relieving Chambers of the Great Pyramid. When assured by a secondary level Egyptian official that he would be notified when access was possible, Sitchin states, "I knew there was a *fat chance* for that." (p. 36) This phrase reveals Sitchin's little recognized sense of humor, and certainly deserves recognition.

INTRODUCTION

12   Brad Silberling, dir. *City of Angels* (Warner Bros. Pictures. 1998), film. Interestingly, the character (played by actor Dennis Franz) whose words are quoted here from this movie's dialogue, was living as a married human, but turned out to be an angel. He had used the *free will* with which angels reportedly are endowed, and elected to leave that unseen angelic realm to live his life on Earth.

13   Compared with the state of knowledge of genetic science on Earth – until recently – the knowledge held by the Other Terrestrials (OT's) was considerably more advanced.

14   Sitchin published two books illuminating those trips: *The Earth Chronicles Expeditions* (2004) and *Journeys to the Mythical Past* (2007). See Bibliography for full citation.

15   See Bibliography for a full list of Sitchin titles.

16   John Casti, *Paradigms Lost: Images of Man in the Mirror of Science* (New York: Avon Books, 1989), p. 42.

17   When early translators found concepts that they could not readily understand, they labeled them *religious beliefs and myths*. These labels are shown, by Sitchin's research, to be misunderstandings. At the time the early scholar's completed their work, cultural and scientific developments did not yet reveal an understanding of the modern concepts and technology that would have permitted more accurate translations.

18   The most well known example is the prodrome launched against the work of Immanuel Velikovsky in the middle of the 20th century. His daughter, Ruth Velikivsky Sharon, deals with this impact in her book, *Immanuel Velikovsky: The Truth Behind the Torment* (2003). Those academics who pilloried Velikovsky's findings published a collection of critical papers, originally delivered at the AAAS, published as: Greenberg, Lewis M. & Sizemore, Warner B. editors. (1978), *Scientists Confront Velikovsky*, published in *Kronos*, Vol. IV, No. 2, Glassboro, NJ: Kronos Press.

19   These Sitchin titles are: *The Earth Chronicles Expeditions* and *Journeys to the Mythical Past* (see Bibliography for additional details).

20   One of the most frequently asked questions posed in Sitchin's in person sessions is, when will the Anunnaki return? He devoted an entire book in 2007 to the evidence in support of the answer to this question. It is titled *The End of Days* (Harper-Collins, 2007). The book's final chapter refers to a cylinder seal that shows an astronaut on Mars communicating with one on Earth with a depiction of a spacecraft between them. Important to the prediction is a pair of fishes on this clay tablet symbolizing the Age of Pisces. The book's last sentence states: "We are still in the Age of Pisces. The Return, the signs say, will happen before the end of our current age." (p. 324)

CHAPTER 1

21   Some scholars, at first, did think they were reading historical material, especially when they found thousands of tablets recording financial and trading records. However, the plethora of unexplainable concepts found in the stories soon contributed to the abandonment of that interpretation for most of the stories in favor of classing them as *myth*.

22   This quote is from the book by Ivan Strenski, a scholar who did in-depth work on Malinowski's writings. Ivan Strenski, *Malinowski and the Work of Myth: Selected and Introduced by Ivan Strenski* (Princeton: Princeton University Press, 1992), p. xiii.

23   This analysis originally is from Malinowski's "Myth in Primitive Psychology," published in Robert Redfield's *Magic, Science and Religion*, re-printed in Ivan Strenski's volume, pp. 77-116.

24   C. G. Heyne *De Origne et Causis Fabularum Homericarun, Commentationis Siocietatis Regiae Scientarium Gottengensis* NF8 (1777) as published in J. W. Rogers, *Myth in Old Testament Interpretation* (Berlin: Walter deGruyter, 1984).

25   Robert Graves and Raphael Patai, *Hebrew Myths: The Book of Genesis* (London: Cassell, 1963), p. 12.

26   J. G. Eichhorn, at the time of his first writing (in 1779), believed that the text of *Genesis 2 & 3* was historical myth, which meant that the events underlying these stories actually happened, but by 1790, he revised his view in favor of a *philosophical* mythical interpretation. J. G. Eichhorn, *Allgemune Bibliothak dur Biblischen Litteratur, 1790-1800* as published in J. W. Rogerson's *Myth in Old Testament Interpretation* (Berlin: Walter deGruyter, 1974), p. 4.

27   Gerhard von Rad, *Genesis* (London: SCM Press, 1961), p. 31 and 32.

28   Ibid., p. 31.

29   George Smith, *The Chaldean Accounts of Genesis – from the Cuneiform Inscriptions* (London: Sampson Iow, Marston, Searle & Rivington, 1880), p. 46.

30   The Anunnaki believed that royal bloodlines were preserved through marriages of brother and sister.

31   These definitions are given most clearly in Sitchin's 2009 publication, *The Earth Chronicles Handbook: A Comprehensive Guide to the Seven Books of the Earth Chronicles* (Rochester VT: Bear & Company, 2009).

32   Louis Delaport, *Mesopotamia* (London: Kegan Paul, Trench, Trubner, 1925), p. 35.

33   Ibid., p. 135.

34   Sitchin, in several of his presentations, explains the seemingly unlikely characteristic of immortality attributed to the Anunnaki

with an illuminating analogy. He says: "Consider you are a housefly on the window, with a lifespan of 3 or 4 days. You look out at the human walking about the kitchen, and you say to another house fly, 'Look at that. He lives *forever*. See, he is immortal.'"

35   Another Sumerian expert, Christian O'Brien, refers to the beings he called the "Annunage" as having "shining faces." One of O'Brien's publications is titled *The Shining Ones*.

36   In King's published transliterations, in the *Enuma Elish*, the word *"ilani"* is translated into English as "god." No doubt this generated considerable confusion to redactors when the same word was used to refer to Enki and Enlil, the leaders of the Anunnaki missions on Earth.

37   In the Introduction to Leonard King's first volume, King states: "The poem embodies the beliefs of the Babylonians and Assyrians concerning the origin of the universe; it describes the coming forth of the gods from chaos...."

38   This translation of the *Enuma Elish: The Seven Tablets of Creation* is taken from L. W. King's translation.

39   See the re-published version of L. W. King's text by The Book Tree publishers, which is readily available.

40   The formation of our solar system was a "battle" between the planets that now comprise it, and another planet that came in from deep space to orbit our Sun, thus making this planet a member of our Solar System. Called in the Creation Epic *Marduk*, it is the planet Nibiru, the home planet of the Anunnaki. To acquire the entire fascinating story as written by Sitchin, the interested reader need only to obtain Sitchin's first book, *The 12th Planet*.

41   In Sumerian, this planet was known as Nibiru.

42   The feminine gender, which the *Enuma Elish* uses to refer to the planet *Tiamat*, likely informs our designation of Earth as "Mother Earth." This gender designation appears in this Sumerian epic.

43   The Moho project drilled to reach the Mohorovicic Discontinuity, the boundary between the earth's crust and mantle. The Moho was named for Andrija Mohorovicic, a Croatian geologist who first proposed the existence of such a discontinuity. The IGY project drilled through the Pacific seafloor at the locations where the Earth's crust was found to be thinnest. The first phase of drilling was located off Guadalupe, Mexico. Five holes were drilled, one which was some 600 feet into the seafloor, and beneath 11,700 feet of ocean. Not only did scientists want to know about the age of the rock through which they drilled, but the composition of the underlying mantle. The scientific information obtained was only partially successful in meeting the project's goals, but it was an ambitious endeavor that did further scientific knowledge. It has been followed more recently by other ambitious explorations of the deep trenches which are located at plate boundaries on the western side of the Pacific basin, and in other global locations where two plates abut. This author does not know of any scientists who are familiar with Sitchin's explanation that ties this information into the ancient wisdom.

44   We find the following description gives us some important facts. "The largest and most southeastern island of the chain, Hawai`i, consists of five volcanoes. Kilauea, Mauna Loa, and Hualalai have erupted in the past 200 years. Lo`ihi, the youngest volcano of the Hawaiian Volcanic Chain, is still about 1,000 meters beneath the ocean's surface. East Maui Volcano, commonly known as Haleakala, on the island of Maui, is the only other Hawaiian volcano to have erupted since the late 1700's." Source: http://hvo.wr.usgs.gov/volcanoes/

45   At Epcot, one of the Florida Disney parks, the regular nightly fireworks show floats a barge containing just such a globe framework that shows the continents as solid material floating on a metal frame's surface.

46   Perhaps this "draining" of the planet's watery covering explains the trilobite fossils found in high altitude locations of mountains, such as the Himalayas.

47   One of the earliest scholars Sitchin studied, Sir Henry Layard, found a site that convinced him that he had discovered

Assyrian regal monuments and cuniform inscriptions from the remains of Ninevah, the great Assyrian capital. From this field work, Layard wrote *Inscriptions in the Cuneiform Character from Assyrian Monuments* in 1851.

48   Joseph Campbell, *The Masks of God: Primitive Mythology* (New York: Penguin Books, 1959), p. 3.

49   Michael Cremo and Richard Thompson, *Forbidden Archeology: The Hidden History of the Human Race* (Los Angeles: Bhaktivedanta Book Publishing, Inc., 1993).

50   This same process of dissemination was used in the early 1950s by Immanuel Velikovsky, who published *Worlds in Collision* and *Earth in Upheaval*. These works were severely criticized by the academic community. One of the criticisms offered against Velikovsky, by Donald Goldsmith, published in the volume titled *Scientists Confront Velikovsky* (1977), is that this approach does not make use of the peer review process that characterizes scholarly work within academia. One can only wonder if it was the public's huge acceptance of Velikovsky's work, or the awareness that the peer review process used in academia would have *prevented* his work from getting into print, that was the basis of the academic consternation.

51   Looking at the official Sitchin website, one can see new announcements of the publication of Sitchin books in languages extant in the global arena.

52   All fourteen publications by Zecharia Sitchin are listed in the Bibliography of this book.

CHAPTER 2

53   Hans Mohr, *Lectures on Structure and Significance of Science* (New York: Springer-Verlag, 1977).

54   Thomas Kuhn, *The Structure of Scientific Revolutions*, 2nd Edition (Chicago: University of Chicago Press, 1970), p. 10.

55   Alan Chalmers, *What is This Thing Called Science?* (St. Lucia University of Queensland, 1976).

56   Debunkers tend to arise from within the body of the population, and typically represent informal experts on topics encompassed by the information. They typically are self-proclaimed experts. Another body of "actual experts" (from the academic arena) takes a similar defensive – or dismissive – stance. The rationale for this latter group's defensive reactions will be discussed below.

57   This is presented as an interpretation of Kuhn discussion, presented in John L. Casti, op. cit.

58   Kramer, publishing in 1966, completed his publication on Sumerian culture prior to Sitchin's first publication.

59   While Kramer did not have exposure to Sitchin's work, Sitchin often referred to Kramer as his "mentor," although the two never met.

60   Joseph Campbell, *The Masks of God: Primitive Mythology* (New York: Viking-Penguin Books, 1959), pp. 143-146.

61   This label, other terrestrials (OTs), is used to refer to the Anunnaki because they came from *another* planet.

62   Though works of fiction, the series of five novels by Jean Auel, called "Earth's Children," provides a plausible, well researched body of explanations of the lifeways of early modern humans of Paleolithic Europe following the retreat of the glaciers. Auel undertook extensive research in the locations where archaeological evidence documents early habitation. Her efforts to understand the paleo-anthropology make her novels a reasonable source for the curious reader to use as a framework for understanding the lifeways of early humans.

63   While invention and trial and error are legitimate modes, they are lengthy processes, inconsistent as explanations of the "suddenness" of the appearance of civilization documented by other scholars.

64   The list of contributions from the Anunnaki to the Sumerians also includes engineering, irrigation, medicine, and even astrology.

65   Sitchin discusses the Anunnaki spaceports and the evidence that corroborates their function as structures built and used by the Anunnaki.

66   Sitchin explains the "creation" process of the *"earthlings"* in three of his books: *The 12ᵗʰ Planet* (pp. 347-354); *Genesis Revisited* (Chapter 8); and *Divine Encounters* (pp. 10-17). Some lines of Sumerian text in a portion of *The Epic of Atrahasis* can be found at: http://www.livius.org/as-at/atrahasis/atrahasis.html. Cylinder seals are small (thumb-sized) artifacts carved with a depiction of something the scribes deemed to be important. When a seal is rolled out on wet clay, it becomes a graphic impression. Thousands of cylinder seals can be found in museum collections displaying Sumerian artifacts.

67   This phrase is the cover subtitle of Sitchin's 1990 publication, *Genesis Revisited*.

68   Notable among the phenomena mislabeled as tombs is the mound called Newgrange, located in the valley of the Boyne River in Ireland.

69   This is a first impression made by my daughter when she viewed her first dolmen while we were traveling in southern Ireland searching for ancient sites, particularly standing stone monuments. It is an apropos (and perhaps accurate) explanation of the purpose of these structures. The capstones typically contain huge amounts of quartz and the capstones are supported by deliberately shaped support stones, as if to delicately balance the "vibrating" capstone.

70   The planet Nibiru is predicted to be on an elliptical orbital path that would enter our solar system at an angle 30-degrees *below* the ecliptic. This southerly trajectory may explain the orientation of the capstone on these dolmen structures. These enigmatic structures may have been poised to vibrate with communication from the planet Nibiru upon its return. Photos show the support (upright) stones to be carved to points that balance the capstone.

71   Martin Brennan, *The Stones of Time: Calendars, Sundials, and Stone Chambers of Ancient Ireland* (Rochester, VT: Inner Traditions International, 1994), p. 10.

72   Michael J. O'Kelly, *Newgrange: Archaeology, Art and Legend* (London: Thames & Hudson, 1982).

73   Hugh Kearns, *The Mysterious Chequered Lights of Newgrange* (Dublin: Elo Publications, 1993), p. 31.

74   The masking plaster and stone work is a recent attempt to support the official Egyptian claim that this structure was built as part of early Egyptian history, and not perhaps 10,000 or more years ago when the Giza plateau was inundated.

75   In Sitchin's book, *Journeys to the Mythical Past*, his first chapter explains an absorbing recounting of his experience in visiting the Great Pyramid when in Sitchin's published words, "... I was almost killed there ..." (*Journeys* book, p. 1).

76   Joseph Ellul, *Malta's Prediluvian Culture at the Stone Age Temples* (Malta, 1988).

77   Ibid., pp. 14-15.

78   Sitchin, Chapter 12, specifically pages 169 and 174.

79   There are numerous sources of the epic, but the one cited most frequently is Stephanie Dalley's translation, *Myths From Mesopotamia: Creation, The Flood, Gilgamesh, and Others.* (Oxford: Oxford University Press, 1989)

80   This site is known in historical writings as the Cedars of Lebonon. These trees had a multitude of uses for most of the ancient and historical cultures that lived around the Mediterranean. Only a few small groves survive today.

81   His goddess mother conferred to him the status of being two-thirds divine. He obtained permission to go to the Landing Place to get on a vehicle that would take him to the abode of the gods.

82   Based on this ancient epic, it is likely that the site called the Landing Place also was a launch site. The epic tells of Gilgamesh awakened by an earthquake-like shaking and the sky darkening. That source's description is remarkably like space vehice launchings in modern times.

83   The mother of Gilgamesh, Ninsun, was Anunnaki, while his father, Lugalbanda (great man Banda) was human. Gilgamesh sought out (and found) Ut-napishtim (Noah), who had been given long life. Ut-napishtim said to Gilgamesh: "since [the gods made you] from the flesh of gods and mankind, since [the gods] made you like your father and mother, [Death is inevitable] at some time, both for Gilgamesh and for a fool." Stephanie Dalley, *Myths From Mesopotamia* (Oxford University Press, 1987, p. 107), as given in her translation of the Epic of Gilgamesh, Tablet X. The second location Gilgamesh was told about was called Tilmun (or sometimes Dilmun).

84   Zecharia Sitchin, *The Earth Chronicles Expeditions* (Rochester, VT: Bear & Company, 2004), p. 173.

85   Conjectures by modern ancient astronaut theorists have suggested some technology that "softened" the stone, thereby allowing it to be precisely shaped. Another conjecture is that some "sound" allowed these objects to be lifted and moved. When the Anunnaki return, perhaps they will explain their techniques.

CHAPTER 3

86   James Mangold, dir. *Kate and Leopold* (Miramax, 2002), film.

87   Interestingly, this author classifies Sitchin into a group of two other 20th century modern heretics whose contributions have a positive effect by moving forward the frontiers of knowledge. The other two are Immanuel Velikovsky and Barbara Thiering.

88   Kuhn, op.cit., on page 24 of his work, draws on Bernard Barber's comments published as "Resistance by Scientists to Scientific Discovery," in the journal *Science,* CXXXIV (1961), 596-602.

CHAPTER 4

89   This is a true statement for those born before 1970. Sitchin's
first book was published in 1976, when those born after 1970 were
starting their formal education.

90   Hans Mohr, op. cit.

91   Ibid., p. 130.

92   John L. Casti, op.cit.

93   Ibid.

94   Case in point, Sitchin's newest book, *There Were Giants Upon
the Earth*, published in May 2010, already is available in the Spanish,
Italian, German and French languages.

95   This work as chief medical officer gained her the epithet of
Nin.ti (meaning Lady who gives Life), Z. Sitchin, *The Earth Chronicles
Handbook* (Rochester, Vermont: Bear & Company, 2009).

96   The conundrum inherent in this evidence is that the Bible
implies that God created humans. When we understand that the
"gods" described by the Sumerian materials were brought into the
Bible narratives under a "one God" construct, we obtain a degree
of clarity. This enlightens us to the sources from which the *Book of
Genesis* was drawn.

97   Admittedly the creationism position claims that God
performed the creation act, but if the God of the *Bible* is a mislabeling
or misinterpretation of the key leaders of the "gods" who came down
to Earth from another planet, then the creating process was from the
Anunnaki, who were referred to as the "gods" (little "g").

98   This is the definition given in Sitchin's book, *The 12th Planet*,
p. 273.

99   Sitchin devotes several pages to the discussion of this
important artifact. See: *The 12th Planet*, pp. 272-279.

100   Ibid., p 274-276.

CHAPTER 5

101   John L. Petersen, *A Vision for 2012: Planning for Extraordinary Change* (Golden CO: Fulcrum Publishing, 2008).

102   We begin this discussion with an important assumption – that we all have accepted the Sitchin material as a plausible, accurate analysis of what the tablets say and accept the interpretations Sitchin has drawn from them. Any who do not accept this assumption will find the following discussion of little use.

103   Robert Fitch & Cordell M. Svengalis, *Futures Unlimited: Teaching About Worlds to Come* (Washington, DC, National Council for the Social Studies, Bulletin 50, 1979).

104   One of the most well-known examples of future thinking is the speech to Congress by John F. Kennedy, delivered on May 25, 1961. The topic is apropos of the overall theme of this book's discussion: The Importance of Space.

105   John L. Petersen, *Out of the Blue: How to Anticipate Wild Cards and Big Future Surprises* (Washington, DC: The Arlington Institute, 1997). Wild cards are low probability, high impact events that catch most people by surprise. Petersen's book discusses selected trends in computer science; social behavior; file expectancy; national and global security; space expeditions; and consciousness research that might converge, or even collide. (These comments are taken from a product review of the book posted on amazon.com.)

106   Some futurists believe that *thought forms* provide a distinctly different way of defining events because by using organized, focused mental energy, we "design" our futures. This concept gives credibility to any conceptual endeavor. It is based on a belief that our futures don't just happen – we construct them.

107   Edward Cornish, "Toward a Philosophy of Futurism," *The Futurist*, vol. 11 (6), pp. 360-381.

108   This list is given in: Norman Henchy, "Building a Framework for the Study of the Future," *World Future Society Bulletin*, Vol. XI, No. 5. September-October. 1977, pp. 1-9.

109   One widely accepted collection of apocalyptic literatures and testaments is: James H. Charlesworth, (editor) *The Old Testament Pseudepigrapha Volume I & II.* (New York: Doubleday, 1983). A notable text within this collection is: *The Book of Enoch.*

110   Norman Henchy, presented in Fitch & Svengalis, *Futures Unlimited: Teaching About Worlds to Come* (Washington, DC, National Council for the Social Studies, Bulletin 50, 1979), p. 15.

111   Zecharia Sitchin, *The End of Days: Armageddon and Prophecies of the Return, the 7th and Concluding Book of The Earth Chronicles* (New York: William Morrow, 2007). This quote is taken from the book jacket.

112   Ibid. These questions are: "Will [the return] be when Nibiru in its elongated orbit returns to our vicinity…? Will there be darkness at noon and the Earth shall shatter? Will it be Peace on Earth, or Armageddon? A Millennium of trouble and tribulations, or a messianic Second Coming? Will it happen in 2012, or later, or not at all?" p. ix.

113   Few Americans know of this document. It can be found at the following web address: http://www.bibliotecapleyades.net/sitchin/sitchinbooks07_05a.htm

114   Interestingly, this tablet is already in widespread circulation. It appears on the cover of the 1996 publication (edited and in part written by Sitchin) that includes the various presentations given at the First Sitchin Studies Day. This book is titled *Of Heaven and Earth.*

115   Sitchin, *The End of Days*, p. 260.

116   Ibid., p. 324.

117   Information on the Age of Pisces in the context of the precession of the 12 constellations of the Zodiac is discussed at:

http://www.halexandria.org/home.htm (this site is attributed to Dan Sewell Ward).

118   Sitchin has stridently pointed out that the return of Nibiru is not associated with the end of the Mayan calendar.

119   This interview was published in *Connecting Link*, Issue 17 and is posted at: www.bibliotecapleyades.net/sitchin/es-sitchin_3a. htm.

120   Most discussions report this destabilization in the context of the melting of the ice sheet, and the calving of huge portions of it into the southern oceans, thereby raising sea levels. This discussion is posted at: http://english.sina.com/technology/1/2008/0114/141437. html

121   See report of the scientific activity of the West Antarctic Links to Sea-level Estimation (WALSE) at: http://www.jsg.utexas.edu/ news/feats/2007/crystal_ball.html and http://www.foxnews.com/ story/0,2933,341428,00.html

122   The consequences of the two parts of the Larson shelf are discussed at: http://www.global-greenhouse-warming.com/Larsen-Ice-Shelf. html

123   A discussion of the relationship between Earth's mantle and crust is found at:
http://www.globalwarmingart.com/wiki/Wikipedia:Earth%27s_crust

124   We will not offer a mathematical probability for this scenario.

125   Two locations experiencing recent earthquakes are in Turkey and Chile. Turkey experienced a serious quake in March 2010 as reported at http://www.csmonitor.com/World/Global-News/2010/0308/Turkey-earthquake-kills-51-scientists-say-earthquake-frequency-not-rising. Chile's February 2010 quake caused human and other widespread impacts, reported at: http:// www.huffingtonpost.com/2010/02/28/chile-earthquake-2010-res_n_479847.html

126   This program's description is given at http://www1. epinions.com/reviews/tele-TV_Channels-All-Discovery_Science

127   Lowman's report is found at: http://denali.gsfc.nasa.gov/ research/lowman/lowman.html

128   We have little historical evidence that volcanic eruptions around the globe were the result of a previous return of Nibiru, with the exception of the eruption of Thera, on what now is the island of Santorini. A caldera was created that today is inundated with Mediterranean waters.

129   We have only to be concerned that the military establishments of the world will provoke deleterious reactions. However, UFO experience has clearly demonstrated that our technology has been rendered unusable when offensive encounters and offensive actions were taken.

130   Sitchin's interview is reported to have appeared in *Connecting Link,* Issue 17, posted at: www.bibliotecapleyades.net/sitchin/es-_ sitchin_3a.htm

131   The three widely viewed movies are: *Independence Day* (Roland Emmerich, dir., 20th Century Fox, 1996), *Aliens* (Ridley Scott, dir., Scott Free Productions, 1979) and the sequel of *Aliens* (James Cameron, dir. Pinewood Studios, 1986).

132   Enki was enjoined by the Anunnaki council from warning humans after their decision to keep the news of the impending deluge from them. So he followed Noah into the temple (Noah was a priest with a regular schedule of prayers). Enki went behind the altar's veil and talked to the wall, giving information on the building of the vessel (ark). The unsuspecting Noah believed he was hearing the voice of God. Enki's intent to save Noah forced this ingenious way of following the council's edict.

133   Sitchin gives a full explanation of the flood event, drawn from the tablets called the *Atrahasis.* See *The 12th Planet,* pp. 276 to 486.

134   One notable event involving U.S. military personnel took place December 26 to 29, 1980 at RAF Bentwaters and Woodbridge air bases. The 81st TAC Fighter Wing was stationed at Bentwaters RAF, a high security facility where nuclear ordinance were stored. During that event, nightly visits of unusual flying objects were witness by U.S. Air Force personnel in Rendlesham Forest. This UFO case is explained and fully documented in a publication by Larry Warren, one of young USAF security officers present at this incident, and Peter Robbins, an investigative reporter. The title of this publication is: *Left at East Gate: A first-Hand Account of the Rendlesham Forest UFO Incident, Its Cover-up, and Investigation* (New York: Cosimo-on-Demand, new edition 2005). A website titled "The Nuclear Connection Project" maintains a list of some 193 reports from 1944 to 1993 of UFO sightings at nuclear site locations. http://www.nicap.org/ncp/ncp-hatch1.htm

135   The data related to nuclear sightings of UFOs are available at the Nuclear Connection Project website, **and appear to** substantiate this assertion.

136   Sitchin, *The End of Days*, p. 93.

137   The scientists involved in performing this analysis have requested anonymity, but their report is scientifically sound.

138   It is known by historians that the Babylonian inhabitants suffered a sudden demise. The structures remained, but the people were gone. If the initial OT nuclear event was inflicted as retribution for seemingly unrepentant sinful behavior (the behavior mentioned in the Bible), to "teach earthlings a lesson," perhaps the aftermath was instructive to them, and they do not want it repeated.

139   This report was published in MUFON's 1994 Symposium Proceedings. However, it must be pointed out that we probably cannot assume benevolence on the part of *all* the ET species currently identified as operating in Earth's vicinity.

140   Some years ago the military of Mexico decided not to attempt to intercept UFOs observed in their airspace. Interestingly, UFO sightings in Mexico abound, and are captured with video cameras by hundreds of citizens.

141   This was reported at the International UFO Congress in February 2010 in a video presentation given by David Sereda.

142   The military decision-makers no doubt also recognized that the technological defenses in their arsenals were defenseless, and rather than admit this to the nation, they pulled back on their aggressiveness.

143   Some reports have come out that secret clandestine research has indeed conquered the gravity barrier, having back-engineered a workable technology from crashed UFOs.

144   Roland Jaffe, dir., *Contact* (Warner Bros. 1997), film.

145   Most readers will recognize this as the command to action of Captain Jean-Luk Picard from the television series, *Star Trek – The Next Generation*.

BIBLIOGRAPHY

Allan, D.S. & Delair, J.B. (1995), *Cataclysm! Compelling Evidence of a Cosmic Catastrophe in 9500 B.C.* Rochester, VT: Bear & Company.

Baigent, Michael. *From the Omens of Babylon: Astrology and Ancient Mesopotamia.* (1994), London: Arkana Penquin Books.

Blamires, Steve. (1992), *The Irish Celtic Magical Tradition.* London: Aquarian Press.

Brennan, Martin (1994), *The Stones of time: Calendars, Sundials, and Stone Chambers of Ancient Ireland.* Rochester VT: Inner Traditions International.

Bulfinch, Thomas. (1979), *Bulfinch's Mythology.* New York: Crown Publishers, Inc.

Campbell, Joseph. (1959), *The Masks of God: Primitive Mythology.* New York: Penguin Books.

Casti, John. (1989), *Paradigms Lost: Trckling the Unanswered Muysteries of Modern Science.* New York: Avon Books.

Chalmers. (1976), *What Is This thing Called Science?* St. Lucia: University of Queensland.

Charlesworth, James H. (eds) (1983), "The Book of Enoch," *The Old Testament Pseudepigraphia Volume I & II.* New York: Doubleday.

Clifton, Chas S. (1992), *Encyclopedia of Heresies and Heretics.* New York: Barnes & Noble.

Cornish, Edward. (1977), "Toward a Philosophy of Futurism," *The Futurist,* Vol. 11 (6), 360-381.

Cremo, Michael A. and Thompson, Richard L. (1993), *Forbidden Archeology: The Hidden History of the Human Race.* Los Angeles: Bhaktivedanta Book Publishing, Inc.

Delaport, Louis. (1925), *Mesopotamia.* London: Kegan Paul, Trench, Trubner.

Evans, M. J. (1996), "The Paradigm Has Shifted: What's Next?' in *Of Heaven and Earth: Essays Presented at the First Sitchin Studies Day.* Escondido, CA: The Book Tree.

Ellul, Joseph. (1988), *Malta's Prediluvian Culture at the Stone-age Temples.* Malta.

Finch, Robert & Svenglis, Cordell. (1979), *Futures Unlimited: Teaching About Worlds To Come.* Washington DC: National Council for the Social Studies.

Freer, Neil. (2000), *Breaking the Godspell: The Politics of our Evolution.* Escondido, CA: The Book Tree.

Graves, Robert & Patai, Raphael. (1963), *Hebrew Myths: The Book of Genesis.* London: Cassell.

Greenberg, Lewis M. & Sizemore, Warner B. editors. (1978), *Scientists Confront Velikovsky: Evidence Against Velikovsky's Theory of Worlds in Collision. Kronos,* Vol. IV, No. 2, Glassboro, NJ: Kronos Press.

Heyne, C. G. (1779), *De Origne at Causis Febularum Homeric run, Commentationis Siocietatis Regiae Scientarium Gottengensis* NF8.

In J. W. Rogers, (1984), *Myth in Old Testament Interpretation.* Berlin: Walter deGruyter.

Henchy, Norman. (1977), "Building a Framework for the Study of the Future," *World Future Society Bulletin.* Vol. XI (5), September-October, 1-9.

Human Potential Foundation (1995), *The Proceedings: When Cosmic Cultures Meet.* Falls Church, VA: Human Potential Foundation.

Kearns, Hugh. (1993), *The Mysterious Chequered Lights of Newgrange.* Dublin: Elo Publications.

King, Leonard W. (1902), *The Seven Tablets of Creation, or the Babylonian and Assyrian Legends Concerning the Creation of the World and of Mankind.* London: Luzac and Co.

Kramer, Samuel N. (1963), *The Sumerians: Their History, Culture, and Character.* Chicago: Chicago University Press.

Kuhn, Thomas S. (1961), "Resistence by Scientists to Scientific Discovery," *Science* CXXXIV, 596-602.

Kuhn, Thomas S. (1970), *The Structure of Scientific Revolutions,* Second Edition, enlarged. Chicago: The University of Chicago Press.

Langdon, Stephen. (1909), *Sumerian and Babylonian Psalms.* New York: P. Geuthner, G. E. Stechert & Co., 1909.

Langdon, Stephen. (1917), *The Epic of Gilgamish. Publications of the Babylonian Section,* vol.10, no. 3. Philadelphia: University of Pennsylvania Museum.

Layard, A. H. (1849), *Nineveh and its Remains.* London: John Murray.

Layard, A. H. (1851), *Inscriptions in the Cuneiform Character from Assyrian Monuments*. London: Harrison and Sons.

Mackenzie, Donald (1915), *Mythology of the Babylonian People*. London: Bracken Books.

Malinowski, Bronislaw , "Myth in Primitive Psychology." In Robert Redfield, M*agic, Science and Religion*, re-printed in Ivan Strenski. (1992), *Malinowski and the Work of Myth: Selected and Introduced by Ivan Strenski*. Princeton: Princeton University Press.

Meaden, Terence. (1999), *The Secrets of the Avebury Stones*. Berkeley CA: Frog, LTD.

Mohr, Hans. (1977), *Lectures on Structure and Significance of Science*. New York: Springer-Verlag.

O'Brien, Christain & O'Brien, B. J. (1999), *The Shining Ones*. London: Dianthus Publishing.

O'Kelly, Michael J. (1982), *Newgrange: Archaeology, Art and Legend*. London: Thames & Hudson.

Petersen, John L. (1997), *Out of the Blue: How to Anticipate Wild Cards and Big Future Surprises*. Washington DC: The Arlington Institute.

Petersen, John L. (2008), *A Vision for 2012: Planning for Extraordinary Change*. Golden CO: Fulcrumm Publishing.

Sharon, Ruth Velikovsky. (2003), *Immanuel Velikovsky: The Truth Behind the Torment. New York*.

Sitchin, Zecharia. (1976), *The 12th Planet: Book I of the Earth Chronicles*. Briarcliff Manner: Stein & Day.

Sitchin, Zecharia. (1980), *The Stairway to Heaven: Book II of the Earth Chronicles*. New York: Avon Books, Inc.

Sitchin, Zecharia. (1985), *The Wars of Gods and Men: Book III of the Earth Chronicles*. New York: Avon Books.

Sitchin, Zecharia. (1990), *The Lost Realms: Book IV of the Earth Chronicles*. New York: Avon Books, Inc..

Sitchin, Zecharia. (1990), *Genesis Revisited: Is Modern Science Catching Up with Ancient Knowledge?* New York: Avon Books, Inc.

Sitchin, Zecharia. (1993), *When Time Began: Book V of the Earth Chronicles*. New York: Avon Books Inc.

Sitchin, Zecharia. (1995), *Divine Encounters: A Guide to Visions, Angels and Other Emissaries*. New York: Avon Books Inc.

Sitchin, Zecharia. (1998), *The Cosmic Code; Book VI of the Earth Chronicles*. New York: Avon Books, Inc.

Sitchin, Zecharia, (2002), *The Lost Book of Enki: Memoirs and Prophecies of an Extraterrestrial God*. Rochester, VT: Bear & Company.

Sitchin, Zecharia. (2004), *The Earth Chronicles Expeditions*. Rochester, VT: Bear & Company.

Sitchin, Zecharia. (2007), *The End of Days: Armageddon and Prophecies of the Return: The 7th and Concluding Book of the Earth Chronicles*. New York: HarperCollins Publishers.

Sitchin, Zecharia. (2007), *Journeys to the Mythical Past*. Rochester, VT: Bear & Company.

Sitchin, Zecharia. (2009), *The Earth Chronicles Handbook: A Comprehensive Guide to the Seven Books of the Earth Chronicles.* Rochester, VT: Bear & Company.

Sitchin, Zecharia. (2010), *There Were Giants Upon the Earth: Gods, Demigods, and Human Ancestry: The Evidence of Alien DNA.* Rochester, VT: Bear & Company.

Sitchin, Zecharia. (Ed. & contributor, 1996), *Of Heaven and Earth: Essays Presented at the First Sitchin Studies Day.* Escondido, CA: The Book Tree.

Strenski, Ivan. (1992), *Malinowski and the Work of Myth: Selected and Introduced by Ivan Strenski.* Princeton: Princeton University Press.

Smith, George. 1980), *The Chaldean Accounts of Genesis: From the Cuneiform Inscriptions.* London: Sampson Iow, Marston, Searle & Riuvington.

Smith, Laurence C. (2010), *The World in 2050: Four Forces Shaping Civilization's Northern Future.* New York: Dutton.

Von Rad, Gerhard. (1961), *Genesis.* London: SCM Press.

ABOUT THE AUTHOR

M. J. Evans earned her doctorate at Syracuse University's Maxwell School in 1978 in the Department of Geography. She focused her early research on environmental perception, perception of mapped information, persistent landscape features, ancient sites, and human cultures and habitats. In her undergraduate degree awarded *cum laude* at Utica College of Syracuse University in 1966, she majored in psychology with a minor in geography. Her doctoral research drew on her undergraduate themes of perception as applied to landscape analysis and human behavior.

From 1969 to 1974, she taught geography at Utica College. Her second academic position was at the newly organized State University of New York's Empire State College, where she taught for 31 years. Her teaching emphasis there focused on adult earners, human geography, earth science, environmental problems, and human impacts on the environment. There she earned the rank of full professor.

Over her academic career, her personal travels took her to ancient sites in Israel, Turkey, Ireland, Great Britain, and France, where she focused on ancient enigmatic landscapes in an effort to tease out their meaning for early peoples. She examined and studied numerous sites in detail, such as Qumran in the basin of the Dead Sea; Newgrange in Ireland; Stonehenge, Avebury and Silbury Hill in southern England; and coastal landscapes in Scotland. To deepen her understanding of the concept of heresy, a topic she explored recently, she studied the Dead Sea Scrolls material, the Templar's history, and traveled to southern France where she visited landscape mysteries in the Rennes le Chateau and Montsegur areas, and the Cathar castles.

Beginning in 1996 she traveled with Zecharia Sitchin and his groups to ancient sites in Greece, and on Santorini and Crete, in addition to explorations in Israel, Italy, and on the islands of Malta.

Dr. Evans retired as Professor Emeritus from her full-time faculty position at SUNY's Empire State College in 2004. She now lives in Syracuse, New York.

ALSO FROM THE BOOK TREE

OF HEAVEN AND EARTH
Essays Presented at the First Sitchin Studies Day

Introduced and Edited by Zecharia Sitchin

Six distinguished researchers, along with Sitchin, present evidence in support of his theories concerning the origins of mankind and the intervention of intelligence from beyond the earth in ancient times.

Presentations:

Zecharia Sitchin, *Are We Alone? The Enigma of Ancient Knowledge*

Father Charles Moore, *The Orthodox Connection*

M. J. Evans, Ph.D., *The Paradigm has Shifted – What's Next?*

Madaleine Briskin, Ph.D., *The 430,000± Years Pulsation of Earth: Is There a 10th Planet Connection?*

V. Susan Ferguson, *Inanna Returns*

Neil Freer, *From Godspell to God Games*

Jose Antonio Huneeus, *Exploring the Anunnaki-UFO Link*

They all agree that Sitchin's work is the early part of a new paradigm -- one that is beginning to shake the very foundations of religion, archaeology and our society in general.

ISBN 1885395174 • 164 pages • 5.5 x 8.5 • paper • $14.95
1-800-700-TREE (8733)   www.thebooktree.com

Lightning Source UK Ltd.
Milton Keynes UK
UKHW020347100821
388593UK00002B/394